FISHING
DIAMOND JIGS
AND BUCKTAILS

FISHING
DIAMOND JIGS
AND BUCKTAILS

TOM MIGDALSKI

Burford Books

Library of Congress Cataloging-in-Publication Data
    Migdalski, Tom.
    Fishing diamond jigs and bucktails / Tom Migdalski.
          p.   cm.
    Includes bibliographical references and index.
    ISBN 978-1-58080-153-9
    1. Jigs (Fishing lures).   2. Saltwater fishing.   I. Title.

    SH449.M54   2008
    799.16—dc22

                                        2008044212

Line drawings by Brittany Haigh.
All photographs by the author unless otherwise credited.

DEDICATION

I dedicate this book to all my fishing partners, but especially to my daughter Maggie for her endless hours of patience aboard many boats, especially ours, while we fished and photographed for this and other written works.

CONTENTS

ACKNOWLEDGMENTS

First and foremost I thank my wife, Carol, for her patience while I commandeered the computer every night and postponed household chores and magazine assignments for many months.

I also thank my father, Ed Migdalski, author of eight books on fishing, for giving me an appreciation for writing, photography and a love of saltwater.

I greatly appreciate the work done by Peter Burford, Pete Barrett, Andy Hahn, Chris Woodword and especially Robert Person for reviewing, editing and offering insights for the outline and manuscript. And I acknowledge Brittany Haigh for creating and providing excellent diagrams.

Recently, as well as over many years, various regional and national experts shared important tips and techniques that contributed to this book. In no particular order, I thank my friends Pat Abate, Matt and Jon Hillyer, George Poveromo, Ed Maturo, Capt. Hal Herrick, Capt. Kerry Douton, Capt. Ned Kittredge, Capt. Al Anderson, Capt. Ralph Allen, Capt. Dan Latham, Capt. Alex Malgieri, Capt. Steve Skevington, Capt. Jim Maturo, Capt. Jim Kaczynski, Capt. Jeff Gutman, Capt. Ricky Mola and Capt. Greg Metcalf.

I especially thank Doug Olander for providing the great West Coast photographs, as well as sharing important information on West Coast vertical jigging techniques.

I'm lucky. I catch a lot of fish, although luck really has little to do with it. I'm successful because I know fish, fishing and saltwater habitats; and it helps to know other fishing experts—many of whom assisted with techniques explained in this book.

But I'm also successful because I fish almost solely with diamond jigs and bucktails. To give you an example of the effectiveness of diamond jigs, days with over 100 bluefish landed aren't uncommon, and I've experienced days when over 30 schoolie bluefin tuna were boated, 70 schoolie striped bass another day and over 50 cod on yet another. Those totals were achieved while fishing only one tide and with only a few anglers aboard. Of course, if you're landing that many fish, you've also hooked and lost many more. No bait can match those types of numbers.

Diamond jigging has many advantages over other popular techniques like trolling and baitfishing. When fishing from a drifting boat, which is how most jigging is done, everything is quiet. There's no drone of motors, and anglers can enjoy easy conversation, the cry of the gulls and the splashing of jumping fish. Better yet, jigging is active fishing. It's not a wait-around, rod-in-the-rod-holder type fishing. You work the lure, feel the hit, set the hook and hold the rod while a big predator burns line off your spool like a tire spinning on ice.

Granted, trolling covers a lot of territory, but when vertical jigging you have already located a precise hotspot like a pinnacle, reef or wreck. Furthermore, whether fishing for salmon, tuna, cod or bluefish, your targeted species is usually bunched up feeding or staging in a large school so you don't need to search for the fish. In fact, some trollers, such as those looking for bluefish or striped bass, troll only as a locater technique and then quickly switch over to jigging once they find a concentration of fish on a given reef.

There's no doubt that baitfishing is productive, but vertical jigging offers several unique advantages. First, you almost never gut hook fish so releasing a healthy fish is easy. Second, pests like dogfish (sand sharks) rarely grab a fast-moving jig compared to constant and annoying dogfish bites on bait. Third, it's much easier and quicker to tie on a jig (usually only once or twice per outing) compared to worrying about storing, cutting, chumming and rigging messy (and sometimes smelly) bait.

Bucktail jigs are equally impressive for catching fish, but in a different way. Bucktails aren't generally responsible for such high numbers of hooked fish like diamond jigs are. Rather, they're the top go-to artificial lure when predators are slow, lazy, off the feed, staging in deep water or when cruising the shallows. Because of a bucktail jig's heavy head and flowing body material, it can induce the most uncooperative fish to strike.

If you had only two types of lures to carry aboard your boat, diamond and bucktail jigs could catch your target fish over 90 percent of the time. The purpose of this book, therefore, is to teach you the major techniques and expert subtleties of diamond jigging and bucktail jigging, which will ultimately enable you to land more fish.

The initial concept of this work started as a book strictly about Northeast diamond jigging—the most popular region and home of that original vertical lure. However, my research quickly confirmed that diamond and similar deep-drop jigs are favored in other areas around the country, especially the West Coast. But publisher Peter Burford and I couldn't stop there because southern anglers favor bucktail jigs in many deep- and shallow-water applications. Thus, what started as a small project became a large one. The book is still weighted toward Northeast diamond jigging, but it now includes detailed jigging information for many popular species off all three coasts.

Because diamond and other heavy vertical jigs are designed for deep-water angling, as are some bucktails, this book is only concerned with boat fishing and doesn't include angling from shore. That subject is well covered in other surfcasting texts, and the material is too broad to try to cover it all here.

After much consideration, I determined diamond-jigging techniques were best categorized and described by targeted species. Bucktails, on the other hand, were best categorized and described by regional environments. Therefore, the diamond jigging chapters are written according to types of fish, whereas the bucktail chapters are written according to types of habitat.

Whether you fish inshore or offshore, I hope this book is useful to you and helps improve your catch. As I write these final words, the wind is light and I'm planning my afternoon trip to jig up some big striped bass over local reefs in Long Island Sound.

Tom Migdalski
June 2008

I
The Lures

DIAMOND AND VERTICAL JIGS

Many styles and variations of diamond jigs exist, but the basic definition of a classic diamond jig is a heavy, bright, four-sided metal lure that is wide in the middle and equally tapered to a dull point on both ends. For the purposes of this book, however, not all vertical jigs will fall precisely into this classification. One such example is the typical Norwegian jig designed primarily for cod. The Norwegian jig is a three-sided metal jig with a thicker, curved lower end and a tapered front-end. Visualize it like an elongated, three-sided teardrop. It performs nearly the same way a true diamond jig does, although it doesn't quite fit the "diamond" definition.

Diamond jigs are popular with many saltwater fishing experts, and these deadly lures have the ability to catch a number of highly-desirable species, including cod, pollock, haddock, bluefish, striped bass, weakfish, rockfish, lingcod, grouper, amberjack, wahoo, tuna and many others.

Anglers can purchase diamonds in a large variety of lengths, styles and weights ranging from ¼ ounce to 32 ounces. Most have a single or treble hook attached to the butt of the lure by means of a fixed, heavy-duty attachment ring, which may or may not have a barrel swivel between the hook eye and the ring. A second attachment ring is affixed at the front end of the jig for tying the line. A few diamond jig configurations feature a single hook with its shank molded into the body of the jig. These are usually small jigs used for species like Atlantic or Spanish mackerel.

The disadvantage of a fixed hook is that a fighting predator can use the hook shank as leverage against the weight of the jig and shake itself free. Also, a free-swinging hook wobbles through the water when fished and simulates the beating tail of a baitfish. Because true diamond jigs have no significant curvature, lip, flex or other means of making them "swim," anglers must work them in one of several jigging techniques to impart fish-attracting action.

Ed Maturo shows why diamond jigs are so deadly. A soft-plastic tube pushed over the hook is especially effective for predators like striped bass and cod.

Why Diamond Jigs?

For overall performance, a diamond jig's naked chrome-plating-over-lead construction is durable and extremely efficient. Diamond jigs are simple, clean, fast and tooth-proof. Using diamonds means no hooks to rebait, no chewed-up surface plugs to discard and no soft plastic or other body materials to replace. Unlike swimming or surface plugs adorned with multiple dangling treble hooks, a diamond jig's body affords a sturdy and safe "handle" for lifting, holding and unhooking feisty fish.

For fishing performance, lures don't get much better. Diamond jigs can plummet in the strongest currents or flutter downward like wounded prey and wobble irresistibly like fleeing baitfish when retrieved. Anglers can also cast diamonds, but vertical jigging is by far the most common method. During white-hot action, such as when working a school of blitzing bluefish, jigs offer a speedy turnaround time. As quickly as you can wrestle a diamond's hook from the maw of a scrappy game fish, you can immediately release the fish and get back to jigging with virtually no wasted time.

Diamond jigs are also relatively inexpensive, especially when compared to some new high-tech lures. A few tackle shops carry seconds

Diamond jigs resemble a wide variety of baitfish such as small Atlantic mackerel. The dimpled finish on this jig simulates scales and reflects more light.

(lures with minor defects) and non-brand name jigs, making purchases even cheaper; but the most expensive diamond jigs are also of higher quality and may, in fact, help you catch more fish.

Besides the varied action of a diamond jig, its other key feature is the shiny, chrome- or nickel-plated finish that's so important for imitating baitfish. The silvery sides of baitfish—such as herring, menhaden, sand eels, silversides, anchovies, shad, mullet and butterfish—reflect the available light, which depends on depth, water clarity and amount of sunlight. On sunny days in clear water, baitfish appear mirror-like, that is, bright silver and highly reflective. In murky water during low-light conditions, however, or in great depths, baitfish become dull. The surfaces of diamond jigs perform the same way, reflecting the available amount of natural light and therefore more closely imitating baitfish than do painted lures.

Selecting Diamond Jigs

Four major elements distinguish diamond-type jigs from each other and determine how you select them: shape, finish, hook configuration and size. I will explore these options for specific species in Part Two; however, here are some basic guidelines to get you started.

Diamond jigs don't have nearly the range of color options as do bucktail jigs. Nonetheless, a well-equipped tackle shop usually stocks both chrome and painted diamond jigs. Painted jigs commonly feature alternating color panels. In other words, two sides will be white and the other two sides will be bright green, red or orange. Such paint is oil-based enamel applied over a lead (or other heavy metal) jig lacking a chrome finish. The paint adheres better to plain lead, and it doesn't make sense to apply chrome plating to a piece of lead and then paint over it.

The paint on diamond jigs is durable, but only to a degree. Rocky bottoms and toothy fish soon scrape off much of the color. The good news is you can easily repaint them, which makes a good off-season project. Selecting painted or chromed jigs is personal preference, but painted lures are sometimes less expensive than their chrome-plated counterparts, and many diamond-jigging experts love them.

Aside from the differing qualities of chrome plating from one manufacturer to the next, there's not much variation in surface appearance among shiny diamond jigs; although you'll sometimes have the option of a smooth chrome finish versus a dimpled or "hammered" chrome finish. Some manufactures also produce gold-colored plating.

A dimpled finish resembles the pattern on a golf ball, except the indentations on a jig are smaller and more numerous. The purpose for the dimples on diamond jigs is to simulate baitfish scales and provide more reflective surface area for increased sparkle.

The latest finishes on jigs are holographic colorations; sometimes coated with clear plastic for extra protection. Some experts aren't convinced one type of finish is significantly better than another; rather, they believe it's how you fish the jig and its inherent action that makes the greatest difference.

One guideline for selecting the size of a diamond jig is to use the smallest jig possible to get the job done. Some less-experienced anglers believe the opposite and think "bigger is better," or "the bigger the bait the bigger the fish." That may be true with live bait, but it doesn't usually apply to diamond jigs. You can work a small lure with more action and less effort. A smaller jig also generates less force when shaken by a hooked fish and therefore reduces chances of the hook wrenching free. A mathematical rule-of-thumb is if you can lightly hold bottom with a 4-ounce diamond jig in 100 feet of water, given identical conditions (wind and current), you'll need an 8-ounce jig to hold bottom in 200 feet of water.

The most important aspect of jig selection is to simulate the size of the local baitfish that predators are keying in on. With the exception of a few large baitfish—like adult menhaden and Atlantic herring—the majority of forage species are small and include juvenile menhaden, young butterfish, thread-fin herring, blueback herring, alewives, anchovies, young shad, sardines, silversides, candlefish, tinker mackerel, round herring, squid and sand eels. You should try to imitate these species with your jig size.

In the majority of situations, 6- to 8-ounce jigs perform well in waters ranging from 100 to 200 feet deep. Three- to 5-ounce jigs are usually heavy enough to maintain bottom in water less than 100 feet deep. These comparatively light weights are especially effective when fished with the new spectra-type super braid lines, which are stronger, thinner, more sensitive and offer less water resistance than comparable-test monofilament lines. Many types of deepwater gamefish are caught using only 6- to 8-ounce jigs, including Atlantic cod, pollock, haddock, tuna, grouper, rockfish and ling cod.

Diamond-style and other vertical jigs also vary in shape. Some are symmetrical, some are weighted toward the head, some are weighted toward the tail, some are long and thin and some are thick along one side and thin along the other. Most of these variations have names, such as Norwegian and Butterfly jigs, and their shapes make a difference in how you fish them and what action they perform.

Hook configuration is an option dependent upon the intended use of the jig. When fishermen work diamond jigs off rugged bottom structure, single hooks are a better choice because they're less likely to snag. Likewise, when targeting toothy critters like bluefish, or when anglers intend to release most of their catch, singles make unhooking safer and easier for both fish and fisherman. When fishing bottom-dwellers over smooth ground or when hunting pelagics in deep water, however, and when such fish are destined for the cooler, treble hooks are preferable because they hook and hold more securely. The latest hook configuration is that of "assist" or "dancing" hooks, which are rigged from the head end of the jig, rather than the tail end, from tethers.

Diamond and vertical jigs are available in a wide variety of designs, weights and hook configurations to fit every angler's needs and resemble most baitfish types. *Photo by Capt. Ned Kittredge.*

History of East Coast Diamond Jigs

John Schmuke, an avid saltwater angler, of the Eastern Toy and Novelty Company, created diamond jigs in the mid-1920s. The business was located in Bridgeport, Connecticut, and that's how the famous

Bridgeport Diamond Jig got its name. Trying to improve his lures, Schmuke bought the Bridgeport Silverware Company in 1929, which until then only manufactured handles for caskets using lead plating, coating and buffering equipment. Over the next few decades, Schmuke's business grew as the design of his jigs was refined and their use began to spread with news of their effectiveness.

In 1955, Bead Chain Tackle Manufacturing—famous for their multi-joint swivels—purchased Bridgeport Silverware, and Schmuke was retained as its director of production. In May 2000, Larry Razza and Capt. Greg Metcalf of Atom Lure Manufacturing (famous for its surface plugs) purchased Bead Chain Tackle and Bridgeport Diamond Jigs from a gentleman named Dana Pickup, adding the jigs to their line of popular Atom fishing lures. Metcalf had been in the fishing tackle industry since 1983, at which point he founded Smoker Baits.

The Uncle Josh tackle company (known for its pork rind baits) acquired the Atom, Bridgeport, Bead and Smoker Baits brands from Atom in April of 2007. "Uncle Josh was the perfect company to take over the fine tradition of our product lines," says Capt. Greg Metcalf,"and the owners of Uncle Josh—Patrick McDevitt and Kurt Kellogg—through acquisitions, have assembled a great product line of old, established companies with excellent product recognition to the fishing tackle consumer in both the salt- and freshwater markets. Each product line will still be marketed under its original label. I stayed on in an advisory capacity during the transition."

Many imitations of the Bridgeport Diamond Jig are on the market, and several others are no longer produced, but the original is still considered superior to the knockoffs. That's because the company uses high-quality lead and buffs their jigs before plating, a process that makes the final jig shinier. Bridgeport Diamond Jigs also use thick, stainless-steel O-rings, which are much stronger and more durable than the thin brass rings used by some manufacturers. Many experts believe that Bridgeport diamonds fish better than their less-expensive counterparts because of their costly and highly-reflective finish, which more closely imitates baitfish in various conditions.

One favorite bygone diamond jig spin-off from the New York/New Jersey area was the AVA. The famous AVA jigs—the company created several styles—were the creation of a man named called Artie, who fished and mated on party boats in the Northeast since he was a boy. He eventually worked in the tackle manufacturing field, where he produced AVA jigs and named them after the first letter in each of three names: his (Artie), his mother's (Viola) and his former wife's (Anita).

Another former knock-off brand, reportedly manufactured until the mid 1980s, was the M&M diamond jig. The name was derived from the brother-and-sister team of Mike and Mary, who produced the lures from their shop in Stratford, Connecticut, and then shipped them to the Bridgeport area for plating. The M&M jigs featured slightly softer edges, stronger O-rings, better finishes and sometimes one hook-size larger than comparable jigs.

Some of the oldest versions of lead lures, such as mackerel jigs, had no silvery plating. Anglers used fine sandpaper to polish the dark-gray tarnish from the bare lead to make them shine. The fresh patina only lasted for one trip in the saltwater, making today's chromed versions comparatively carefree.

Diamond Jig Variations

Countless versions of diamond and vertical jigs are on the market. However, one of most popular variations of the four-sided diamond jig is a three-sided lure that is weighted more heavily toward the hook end; thus, not perfectly symmetrical. The top brands of these wonderful jigs, which are ideal for trolling, vertical jigging and casting, have included the Solvkroken, Sumo Chrome Banana, VI-KE, S&G VK and Viking. Here are some interesting facts about these deadly three-sided lures:

Cod jigs differ in their design and weight. The most well known of these lures is the three-sided Norwegian jig. Commercial cod fishermen have hand-lined these lures for many decades off Norway, England, Iceland, Canada, Maine and Massachusetts. The VI-KE company eventually produced these lures in the U.S. and made them popular with recreational fishermen. VI-KE jigs were manufactured by Bead Chain Tackle (maker of Bridgeport Diamond Jigs), then produced by Atom Lure Manufacturing and now by Uncle Josh. VI-KE cod-style jigs are available in sizes ranging from 4 to 24 ounces, and they are the original U.S.-made Norwegian-style jig. A few other lure makers in the U.S. also produce Norwegian-type jigs, sometimes in even greater weights and almost always with treble hooks. The knock-offs are named similarly, and you may see them labeled as VK, VKE or Viking.

The S&G VK jig is an example of the classic, but more slender, three-sided diamond cod jig. Originally made by Bob Sparta and Gary Goldstein (S&G) in Brooklyn, NY, starting in the early 1970s, the two buddies reportedly moonlighted as commercial anglers off Long Island, NY. Around 1990 they stopped producing the jigs. Unfortunately, the S&G jig's inheritor had no intention of making new molds, so it appears Sparta and Goldstein's original casting is gone.

Other three-sided diamond jigs include AVA jigs and the Chrome Banana jig. AVA's three-sided jig was similar to the VI-KE but not identical. The smaller versions were popular for false albacore and bonito in the Northeast.

The Chrome Banana, while not an exact copy, is Sumo Tackle's version of S&G VK and VI-KE jigs. The Chrome Banana is three-sided, slightly more banana shaped and constructed of solid brass with thick chrome plating. The lure is rigged with a single Siwash hook and sports swivels on both ends, which is an important feature for preventing fish from twisting and leveraging against the weight of the lure and tearing out the hook. Chrome Bananas are available from 3 to 10 inches long and ¾ to 24 ounces. They're a good choice for bluefish, cod, tuna, rockfish, lingcod, grouper and striped bass, among others.

Solvkroken cod jigs, made in Arendal, Norway, appear to be the original Norwegian cod jig. They're imported by U.S. and Canadian tackle distributors and range in size from 9 to a massive 43 ounces. Although more expensive, many cod experts consider these stainless-steel Norwegian jigs superior to some chrome-plated or hand-painted Norwegian-style knockoffs because of their durability, heavy-duty hardware and polished shine.

Many other very good Norwegian-style jigs are produced by small companies in the Northeast, and they all have their dedicated followers. Two of the favorites are the Lavjig and Danny Angerman jig. Popular sizes range from 12 to 16 ounces and are worked off the bottom in the same fashion as other cod lures.

Norwegian-style lures, like other three-sided jigs, are thicker and wider at the hook end and tapered at the front end. Additionally, one of their three sides is sharply curved inward at the base. This unique, base-heavy shape allows the jigs to drop quickly through water column when free-spooled with a slight amount of line tension, keeping the jigs in a relatively vertical position. Once jigged off the bottom with a yo-yo motion, however, the jigs fall with a fluttering action similar to a crippled baitfish or a spawning herring, which undulate, flutter and dart around while mating and depositing milt or eggs on a gravel seafloor. In other words, the more horizontal action a vertical jig displays the more enticing its appeal.

West Coast Iron Jigs

"Irons" are very popular terminal tackle choices of West Coast jig fishermen. The term iron refers to various heavy lures made of die-cast zinc, lead or other alloys and manufactured by famous brands such as Sumo, Tady, UFO, Salas and Iron Man, and others. Some anglers also categorize the new Japanese-style deep-drop and flutter lures as irons. Irons are designed to be dropped vertically for yo-yo or speed jigging for amberjack, yellowtail, lingcod and many Pacific gamefish. The West Coast term for fishing iron jigs is "throwing" iron because anglers often cast them away from the boat either to reach breaking fish or to assist in achieving a more vertical drop from a drifting boat.

Perhaps the most classic West Coast iron jigs are referred to as "Candy Bar" jigs, this type of lure—somewhat resembling a flattened diamond jig—has been a mainstay of West Coast and Baja anglers for years. They are usually made from solid-cast metal such as aluminum, zinc, copper or lead and are rigged with heavy-duty Siwash or treble hook. These jigs are very durable and are ideal for deep yo-yo style jigging for ling cod, grouper, snapper, yellowtail, amberjack, wahoo and tuna.

In the spring of 2006, two legendary names in California's jig-making history united when the Tady Lure Corp. acquired all assets of the esteemed Candybar Lure Co. According to Jim Shimizu of Tady Lures, his company was very pleased that one of California's first iron jig makers was now under their umbrella. Bob Manning, the son of the Candybar's inventor, had retired and stopped making jigs several years ago, which made availability scarce. Tady purchased the remaining inventory of raw, unfinished jig blanks, along with the jig mold and the original wooden mold sample. Their first batch was strictly bare aluminum. Tady Lures now manufactures Candybars in their three original sizes, including the 112, which is similar to the Tady 45; the 200, which is similar to the Tady 4/0; and the 150, which is similar to the Tady A1.

Another example of these jig types is made by Sumo Tackle, which has a selection of casting and deep-water jigs that are popular with offshore fishermen pursuing pelagic or bottom species. Sumo 6 and 7X iron jigs are classic West Coast-type jigs, but they have a variation. Sumo modified their Candybar jigs by applying a luminescent paint to the back side of the lure. These lures are made from a solid one-piece metal and rigged with heavy Mustad treble hooks.

Bar, hex bar and other iron jigs are simplistic lures made from sections of metal bars, cut at an angle at both ends to increase action. The bars may be lead-filled pipe or solid stock, commonly ranging in size from 2 to 16 ounces and 4 to 7 inches long. Lure makers drill holes in each end to attach the line and a hook. These jigs are seldom used on the East Coast but are a mainstay on the West Coast for deep-feeding fish like lingcod, calico bass and yellowtail, which may feed in waters 150 feet deep or more.

It's a lot easier to make your own bar jig than to attempt to create a diamond or VI-KE jig, however, if you do wish to make your own diamonds, a variety of jig molds are available from Do-It Molds at www.do-itmolds.com. First, obtain sections of narrow-diameter metal tubing, such as copper, aluminum, chrome or galvanized pipe. Stop at a tire shop and ask for a few pounds of discarded lead weights from the tire-balancing process. Melt the lead in a well-ventilated area, using extreme care to keep the product away from moisture and not breathe the fumes.

While wearing appropriate eye and hand protection, fill the pipe stock with the molten lead and let cool. Once cold, cut the pipe to the desired length, usually 6 to 10 inches, at a 45-degree angle at both ends. Drill holes in each end and attach large, stainless-steel split-rings for the line and hook. Coat your lures with a base of metal primer and, once dry, apply bright enamel paint. You can make the jigs more attractive and enticing by adding decals like eyes, holographic fish-scale-type patterns or glow strips.

2

BUCKTAIL JIGS

A bucktail jig is any one of an extensive variety of artificial lures possessing a heavy metal head—usually lead—molded around the front end of a single-hook shank. Unlike diamond jigs, however, bucktail jigs are equally popular in both fresh and saltwater fishing.

A second type of hook configuration, used almost exclusively in saltwater, is the "swing-hook" style, in which the head is molded around a protruding O-ring where the hook is then fastened. The free-hook arrangement has several advantages over the set hook design. For example, the free-swinging hook allows the shank to move independently of the heavy head, thus preventing fish from using it as leverage against the weight and shaking free. Swing hooks can be replaced when rusty, keeping the body material from staining brown. They also allow for a more natural and linear presentation of the body material and teasers. Finally, many experts believe that swing-hook jigs are easier to dislodge when snagged on bottom structure.

The eye of a bucktail jig—a second attachment eye ring where the line is tied—protrudes from the front of the head at a 45- or 90-degree angle, letting the angler impart better jigging action and reducing bottom snags. The shank of the hook is never fished bare and is always dressed with permanently-affixed animal hair (hence the name "buck" tail, as in deer, but calf tail is also used). However, synthetic hair—usually made from bright nylon—is much more durable and is now also commonly used. Experienced fishermen usually tip their jig hooks with a strip of pork rind, soft plastic or natural bait trailer for additional action and/or scent.

A bucktail's body material, regardless of its composition, is traditionally tied on facing rearward. However, a variation of the bucktail jig, called a parachute jig or "'chute," uses long nylon fibers facing both forward and rearward for added pulsating action, which is popular for slow trolling. Parachute jigs, although not technically bucktail jigs, are extremely effective, and I will discuss them in Chapter 24 on wire lining.

Anglers can purchase bucktail jigs in a wide range of weights, sizes, styles and colors. Head shapes vary greatly, and saltwater types include ball, bullet, oval, keel, football, pot belly, banana, bean, pop-eye, stand-up and mushroom. Much of the selection process is based on experience and preference; however, different head shapes do have somewhat different functions, and their selection is dictated by fishing technique and expected water conditions. Ball, bullet, open-mouth and football shapes are popular in saltwater because they are compact and heavy, thus allowing them to sink fast, carry big hair bodies and hold the bottom better.

Although synthetic body fibers are very durable, real bucktail is still an excellent material because it has a natural taper to each strand that provides tantalizing movement in the water. Natural hair allows water to flow over and through the jig with less drag to achieve optimal action. Micro-currents actually move or "swim" through and around the hair collar where it's attached near the head, then continue rearward to the tail. The hairs respond to the currents, and a moving jig instantly becomes lifelike.

Once you begin studying the many jigs hanging on tackle shop displays, you'll quickly realize that not all bucktail materials are identical. Besides the obvious difference in dye color, real hair can be long or short, straight or wavy, soft or coarse and thick or sparse. The craftsman selecting and tying on the fibers carefully controls those characteristics. Seasoned anglers search through jig brands for the material length, color, thickness, head shape and weight best suited for expected conditions.

Because the advantage of natural bucktail hair is its taper, which allows it to flow so enticingly, you should never shorten the overall length of your jig by cutting off part of the tail. You'll remove the taper and end up with a stubby, unrealistic lure that creates abnormal drag when fished. How many baitfish have you seen with a blunt, squared-off end like a cut cigar? You're better off simply buying a smaller jig. The tapered trait of natural animal hair has yet to be successfully copied with synthetic fibers. Real bucktail jigs offer an action and appearance that is still hard for technology to replicate.

Why Bucktail Jigs?

A bucktail jig is one of most popular, productive and versatile lures ever created. That's why survival kits, including those assembled by the Navy, contain a length of fishing line and one or more bucktail jigs. Bucktails can be deep jigged, trolled, drifted or cast.

Maggie Migdalski proudly shows that bucktail jigs are so easy to use that even kids can catch big fish with them. This large weakfish fell for a bucktail Maggie hopped along the up-tide side of reef in Long Island Sound.

For less experienced anglers, bucktail jigs may appear to have many drawbacks: They don't glitter or shine. They aren't innovative or technologically advanced. They don't require extensive practice. They aren't very pretty. They don't produce breathtaking top-water strikes. And they don't look like a real baitfish. So why should anyone keep a selection of bucktail jigs in his tackle box? The answer is "simple." Bucktail jigs are a simple lure that are simple to fish yet achieve some of the most impressive catches of any artificial lure on the market.

Although bucktail jigs don't imitate any particular species, they somewhat resemble and can move like most types of forage. If pressed to pick one type of prey that bucktail jigs resemble, it would be squid—one of the all-time favorite forage foods of most gamefish. However, a bucktail may also appear like a grass shrimp, small lobster, mantis shrimp or any of a wide variety of baitfish. It doesn't look exactly like any one thing, but it looks like everything. That's why it belongs in your tackle box.

Selecting Bucktail Jigs

Bucktail jigs are available in a dizzying array of dazzling colors: hot pink, chartreuse, royal blue, blood red, purple, yellow, green, black and several others, either alone or in color combinations. All these varieties may be as much to catch fishermen as to catch fish. You could easily decorate a Christmas tree with them.

There's no secret formula to determine the best bucktail jig color, but with experience you'll develop preferences. I believe most of your bucktail jigging success will come from how and where you fish, rather than what psychedelic shades you choose. That said, however, there are a few basic go-to colors that will produce fish a majority of the time. For daylight fishing, your best all-purpose color is white, followed closely by chartreuse or the popular combination of chartreuse and white. For night fishing, black and dark purple are your best bets.

Predators feed by grabbing their prey from behind, the side or underneath. Rarely do gamefish attack baitfish downward from above. That means the predominant color predators key on is white. Baitfish have dark dorsal sides to camouflage them from big fish looking down toward a dark bottom. White undersides wrap upward around baitfish to camouflage them from big fish looking up against the bright sky. Squid, the forage species bucktails most resemble, are also mostly white. Therefore, if you could only afford one type of jig in your tackle box, carry several sizes in white.

You also have a better chance of catching fish when your hook is in the water. That means you'll usually catch more fish by keeping a white jig in the water than by wasting time constantly switching jigs trying to determine the hot color for the day. Color selection has some merit, and I'll discuss more about choices in the bucktailing chapters as they pertain to specific species.

The reason black or dark purple lures are effective after dark is because baitfish appear as silhouettes at night. With no sunlight to reflect off them, they actually look dark against the lighter watery background, which is illuminated by sparse amounts of ambient light from the night sky. Although a novice would think the opposite is true, choose light colors during the day and dark colors at night.

The other major factors when choosing bucktails are head weight and hook size. You won't have much choice with the hook size, except for those you change out, when possible, because the manufacturers match an appropriate size hook to weight of the lead head and its intended use. In other words, small jig heads come with small hooks, and large jig heads come with large hooks.

Two of the most popular categories of bucktails, especially in the Northeast, are termed rip splitters and jetty casters. To novices the main differences are the size and color of the jig, but the real difference is how much hair is tied behind the head. The jetty caster-style is constructed with a lot more hair, which creates a jig that swims higher in the water than a rip splitter of the same weight. This means you can use a ½-ounce or heavier jetty caster than you could fish with a rip splitter-type bucktail. The additional weight allows you to make longer casts and work the jig closer to the bottom if encountering strong currents or big waves. Conversely, when plying deeper water with strong tides, like in rips, rip splitter-types are more efficient because they cut through the current to reach the fish with less resistance.

As with diamond jigs, and what I'll emphasize periodically through the book, you should select the lightest weight possible to obtain the desired results. The lighter the jig, the easier it is to work properly and the better the action. Also, the lighter the jig the more difficult it is for a fish to leverage against and throw the hook during head shakes.

When selecting a jig for the expected conditions, remember these basic guidelines: Always use a heavier bucktail when the water is deep, the current is fast, the surf is large or the drift or troll is fast. Likewise, you should always use lighter weights during less demanding conditions.

If fishing sand flats, for example, you need a jig you can cast a long way to shy fish. You may think you'd need a heavy jig to travel the greatest distance, but the opposite is true; a lighter jig won't make as much commotion when it lands, and it offers better action across the sand bottom, especially when far away. You'll be able to fish correspondingly lighter tackle, which means using lighter line enabling longer casts. You will be able to use lighter leader for better action of the lighter jig, which will be less visible to spooky fish. Fish on a sand flat aren't likely to pull your line around boulders or mangrove roots, so you can get by with light tackle and light jigs for the best all-round presentation and still make long casts. So lighten up!

With a few exceptions, bucktail jigs are designed to be worked along the bottom. Fish with whatever weight is necessary to maintain bottom contact, given the current speed, depth, line resistance, surf resistance and boat drift speed—but not an ounce more. For example, in water only 10 to 20 feet deep with a light current 1½ ounces may work perfectly; however, when in water 50 to 100 feet deep with a strong current you may need a 4- to 6-ounce jig.

History of Bucktail Jigs

Bucktail jigs are probably at least as old as diamond jigs are, but their exact date of invention is difficult to pinpoint. The forerunner of the bucktail jig is likely a bucktail fly that was weighted to achieve casting distance, depth or both. In fact, a bucktail fly may simply have been fastened to a lead weight, making it similar to today's "new" fluke ball lures. Bucktail flies were first used in the United States in the early part of the 20th century. In saltwater, they were originally used in the Pacific Northwest for salmon, the Northeast for striped bass and the Southeast for bonefish and tarpon.

A half-century ago, all bucktail jigs were designed and intended for saltwater use, but with the introduction of spinning gear, small versions of bucktail jigs—sometimes weighing only a fraction of an ounce—were created for freshwater fishing. Today, they remain one of the most reliable lures for both fresh and saltwater.

3

JIGGING ENVIRONMENTS

Tides and Currents

How good is your knowledge of the tides? Try this simple test to find out: Do you think apogee means saying you're sorry, perigee means an ancestral line of purebred animal, and amplitude means how high a plane flies? Do you think flood only happens when it rains too much, and slack only happens when you lose a fish? Can you explain ebb, neap, and mean low water? Do you know how many minutes the high tide advances each day or how tide and current differ? All these terms influence bucktail and diamond jig fishing.

Tide is defined as the vertical rise and fall of water, and current is the horizontal flow of water. Amplitude is the distance between the high and low tide marks. In most saltwater fishing a strong correlation exists between the stages of the tide and fish-feeding activity.

Currents, which are the movements of water, are easier to see in smaller areas, such as bays and estuaries, and they're usually swifter there than at sea because the water volume is pushed through a narrow area, which forces it to speed up. The wind can also affect tides and currents by its influence on the surface, but the moon ultimately determines when the tide moves and its amplitude.

As you probably know, tides are caused by the moon's gravitational pull as it orbits the earth, combined with the earth's rotation along its axis. The pull forces the water to surge on both sides of the earth, raising and lowering the water level twice daily. The tide becomes high approximately every 12 hours and 25 minutes, and each day the high tide occurs about 50 minutes later than it did the previous day. Spring tides occur when the sun and moon are in line with earth on the new and full moon. Neap tides occur when the sun and moon pull at right angles on the first and last quarter of the moon. Spring tides are extreme, and neap tides are moderate.

Because the moon revolves around the earth in an elliptical pattern it pulls against the oceans with varying intensity. When the moon passes at its nearest point it creates perigee or extra high and low tides. When it passes at its farthest point it creates apogee or unusually light tides. Fishing improves on certain moon phases. Keep a notepad to record fish activity at the various stages and velocities of the tide in your area. Usually, the best fishing with jigs occurs within the four hours of peak current flow between slack water periods.

Tides flood when they come in and ebb when they go out. A tide flooding into an estuary increases fish feeding activity because it carries new forage from the ocean. As tides surge over flats they provide more water for fish to move in and feed where they couldn't at low water. Conversely, the ebb draws fish from the shallows as the water thins, but it stimulates feeding at estuary mouths because it sweeps forage down from the shallows to waiting predators. Ebb tides are usually warmer tides because the sun has had time to heat the waters inshore. Flood tides are usually cooler because they carry in water from deeper areas offshore.

Be wary of obstructions as the tide drops. While structure attracts forage and predators, it also poses a threat to your motor and hull. Many a craft has grounded on a rock, ledge, shoal or sandbar on a falling tide. Navigational charts list mean low water in feet, which tells you the average minimum depth to expect. During a moon tide or windy conditions, however, the water level might be several feet lower than indicated.

Estuaries, including tidal creeks, rivers, bays and harbors, offer a mix of fresh and saltwater. An enormous amount and variety of forage, such as baitfish, sea worms, shrimp, eels and crabs make their home in estuaries. On the ebb tide many of these morsels are swept into the coastal waters to meet waiting predators. Snook, sea trout, bluefish, weakfish and striped bass all cruise river and creek mouths waiting for the falling tide to carry nervous bait from their rapidly diminishing upstream sanctuary.

Numerous other natural and manmade structures create inshore fishing environments, including breakwalls, jetties, piers, points, islands, keys, mangroves and channels offer terrific fishing as the tide courses along or around them. I will discuss these in greater detail in the various bucktail jigging chapters.

Fish always face into the current so they can easily maintain stability and inhale water. It's also the best position to smell, see and intercept forage moving down tide. Therefore, the best way to present your jig is down or across the current. Baitfish seldom swim uptide, and gamefish may ignore an offering being dragged against the current by your line.

Rips and rocky shorelines are both ideal environments to work diamond jigs and bucktails. Scenic views are a bonus while jigging. This piece of challenging water and the historic lighthouse are located on the west side of Plum Island in the eastern end of Long Island Sound.

Rips

Rips deserve special attention in a book on diamond and bucktail jigging for several reasons: First, jigs are designed for the unique conditions of rips. Second, rips require greater knowledge and are more challenging to fish than typical "flat" water. And, third, rips attract and hold many species of predators making them reliable go-to hotspots. Ask any top anglers or charter captains about their favorite fishing locations and most will mention rips.

Without rips, countless areas along the coast wouldn't hold nearly as many gamefish. That's because rips provide three of the most important elements in fishing: structure, strong tidal flow and concentrated forage. But, to be successful at catching any of the numerous species that inhabit rips, you must first understand their abrupt bottom contours and how currents move over them.

Strong tides create rips when water flows over large obstacles like ledges, reefs, boulder fields, banks, shoals and bars. As a swift current hits such a structure, the hump forces water to compress and speed up as it sweeps over it. That's because the water flowing through the narrower area *over* the structure must keep pace and meet with the

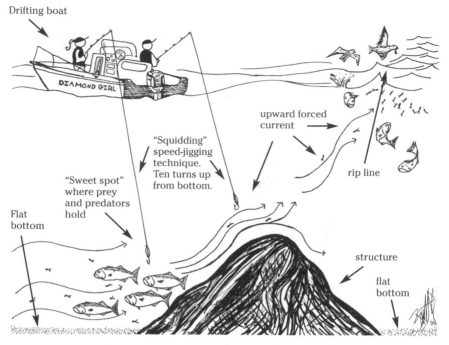

Labels in image:
Drifting boat
DIAMOND GIRL
"Squidding" speed-jigging technique. Ten turns up from bottom.
"Sweet spot" where prey and predators hold
Flat bottom
upward forced current
rip line
structure
flat bottom

Diamond Jigging In Front of a Rip Line

unobstructed, deeper water flowing *around* the structure. It's the same principle that causes water to jet through a constricted nozzle instead of gurgling out of a large, open hose.

A series of standing waves, called a rip line, form when the faster, upwelling water collides with the deeper, slower water behind the structure. This is easy to spot because the water ahead (upcurrent) of the rip line is relatively calm, while the water behind (downcurrent) of the rip line is very choppy and roiled.

Near the bottom, this up-surging motion causes a vacuum-like effect—the same way an airplane wing achieves lift from air rushing over it, and the same reason roofs are lifted off houses during hurricanes. Immediately ahead of the reef, however, is a pocket of calmer, slower water. This comparatively quiet area is known as the sweet spot. Since it takes time and distance for the upwelling water to reach the surface, the sweet spot is located a short distance—depending on the depth and current speed—in front of the rip line, not directly beneath its leading edge. Hence the reason to fish jigs in the calm water uptide of the rip line and not in the rip itself.

Gamefish hold in the sweet spot to conserve energy and ambush baitfish that gather there to seek shelter and feed on organisms stirred off the ocean floor. Some types of predators, like bluefish, will also chase prey up through the water column and grab it near the surface, usually just in front of the rip line. Envision a trout holding along a protective boulder in a river and then following newly-hatched nymphs to the surface before inhaling them. In that example, fly fishing experts would use a sinking line and wet fly rather than a floating line and dry fly. This is an ideal reason for working diamonds, and that's why vertically-retrieved jigs are so much more effective than surface plugs in this situation.

Inexperienced anglers see a few surface breaks along a rip line and immediately think, "the fish are feeding on top." That's not a good assumption. It's like looking at an iceberg: You only see the tip of the activity on the surface while 98 percent of the action is happening underneath. That's exactly why diamond jigs will significantly outfish surface lures in these circumstances.

Rips can form in shallow or deep water. To locate fish-holding rips in your area you don't need to find a particular depth, but rather examine a chart and pinpoint spots where the depth rises and falls abruptly, preferably from structures running diagonally or perpendicularly to the current flow. The best spots usually appear where relatively flat ground suddenly meets a natural bottom contour with significant vertical relief, such as a reef or shoal, over which a strong current passes.

Most shallow reefs are easy to find because they're marked with navigational aids, but deeper reefs not marked with warning or navigational buoys are also easy to spot by their signature rip line during a moving tide. The size of the waves along the rip can range from a subtle few inches to 2 or 4 feet or more depending on the current force, rate of depth change and wind direction and speed. A strong wind opposing a stiff current will create a much larger rip line than when the current and wind are moving in the same direction. The reason is because the surface water flow collides with the wind and "heaps up" at the same spot where the fast water meets the slow water over the peak of the reef. These situations cause extremely hazardous conditions for small craft, especially when drifting into a rip stern-first.

Although most reefs, and therefore rips, are located anywhere from a half mile to several miles offshore, shore points tapering to subsurface spits often create rips fishable from a boat. These landmasses can originate from the mainland and are often found off the tip of coastal islands. The current pushing over these sometimes-treacherous shallows creates prime predator habitat you can fish with jigs all the way to shore assuming, of course, you have enough water under your hull.

Many inshore reefs are marked by navigational aids; however, those reefs not designated are harder for average anglers to locate and often receive less fishing pressure as a result. They are excellent places to work with either diamond jigs or bucktails.

The size of the rip line has no correlation to the fish activity below, and some rips showing only the slightest riffles on top may be stacked with fish like lobsters in a Maine clambake. On days when predatory fish are chasing baitfish to the surface, anglers can spot working birds from a considerable distance, and these birds often reveal the location of a productive reef. Once the tide slacks, however, rip lines vanish with no indication of what lies beneath except what shows on your depthfinder. Unfortunately, when rips stop showing the fishing action also stops.

The strong current in rips causes baitfish to cluster, which makes feeding easier for predators. Conversely, during slack tide baitfish face different directions and scatter, making it more difficult for predators to track and target them. Likewise, gamefish scatter, rest and stop feeding during slack water. That's why fishing is often at its best during the first hour of hard tide movement. The prey resumes their schooling tendencies, and the predators are hungry again after their rest. But this timing doesn't apply to all fish.

Aggressive gamefish like bluefish, weakfish, striped bass, bonito and false albacore, feed best when baitfish are tightly packed and panicked, and that happens during peak tidal flow when rip lines are at their most prominent. That means the best fishing period for jigging is during the three middle hours of the tide.

Likewise, full and new moon tides, as described earlier, have greater amplitude than average and therefore carry faster currents. The current is faster because more water must move through a given area in the same amount of time, approximately every six hours. This increased tidal flow often increases baitfish and predator movement and feeding. As a result, bigger tides can produce new hotspots, often on reefs with lower vertical profiles, which are usually devoid of fish during half-moon tides. For those anglers willing to put in the extra work to search for and experiment on these unknown structures the results can be remarkable during moon periods.

Banking on Banks

Banks produce many of the greatest catches of major offshore species like cod, pollock, haddock and halibut. Pelagic species like tuna are also attracted by the unique ecosystems of banks. One of the largest and best known rises of the ocean floor is the Grand Banks located northeast of New England. Banks, however, can be found off many areas of the continental shelf around the United States.

Envision banks as gigantic shoals, generally located offshore, composed of any combination of sand, silt, rocks, clay and gravel. Some banks are natural contours of the ocean floor caused by plate tectonics 200 million years ago when the oceans first formed. Others were formed by glacial deposits. Some banks were once dry land, which were then covered by ocean water when the glaciers melted and raised sea levels by about 300 feet.

The famous Stellwagen Bank in the Gulf of Maine is an example of the latter two conditions. During the last glacial period, over 400 feet of sediment was deposited over a foundation of bedrock and coastal plain strata, causing a huge shoal about 20 miles east of Massachusetts. The shallowest areas on Stellwagen Bank range from 70 to 120 feet deep and were therefore possibly 200 feet above the water 20,000 years ago. In fact, ancient mammals roamed across the bank, as evidenced by artifacts such as a mastodon tooth recovered by a commercial draggerman. What makes banks so attractive to fish aren't their fascinating origins, but rather their comparatively shallow water and the way ocean currents move over their structure.

Because banks are so shallow, at least compared to the surrounding ocean basins, sunlight is still able to penetrate the water to the bottom. This allows phytoplankton to survive in normally inhospitable offshore locations. Plankton are minute life forms—animal or plant—that can remain suspended in the upper water column but cannot actually swim. Phytoplankton are simply plant plankton that rely on sunlight and ocean nutrients to achieve photosynthesis. Zooplankton are animal plankton—or the tiniest marine animals—that survive on phytoplankton. Similar to the function of land-based plants like trees or grass, phytoplankton are at the bottom of the oceanic food chain.

In other words, phytoplankton are the primary food source for zooplankton, and zooplankton are the main forage for numerous important baitfish, such as sand eels, herring and menhaden. Larger predators, including cod, pollock, haddock and tuna feed on these baitfish. Thus, phytoplankton require the sunlight available on banks to survive, and their presence then attracts baitfish and sport fish. Even though you can barely see these organisms, they are responsible for the outstanding fishing that banks provide.

Some banks are quite large, extensive underwater plateaus that rise abruptly from the ocean floor. Due to their steep vertical relief, banks force water currents to be altered in a phenomenon known as upwelling, which occurs when deep ocean currents and changing tidal flow hit these massive structures and are pushed up and over the walls of the plateaus. The positive effect from this motion is to carry nutrients stirred from the ocean floor into the shallower water above the banks. Phytoplankton thrive in bank waters because of the available sunlight for photosynthesis and the micronutrients, which they consume as food.

Thermoclines and Temperature Breaks

A temperature break, also called a thermal break or convergence zone, is a sudden and distinct change in sea-surface temperature. Find these vertical temperature boundaries by watching your water-surface temperature gauge when running offshore. An abrupt change in water color, such as from green to blue, can also indicate a temperature break and is often accompanied by birds, seaweed and rips.

These zones develop when warm, offshore water collides with cooler inshore water. A temperature boundary forms where the two water masses meet and make an excellent place to troll and jig for tuna and other pelagics, such as marlin and dolphin, because the breaks attract baitfish. Fishermen can also locate warm-water eddies and temperature breaks from their computer via satellite imagery.

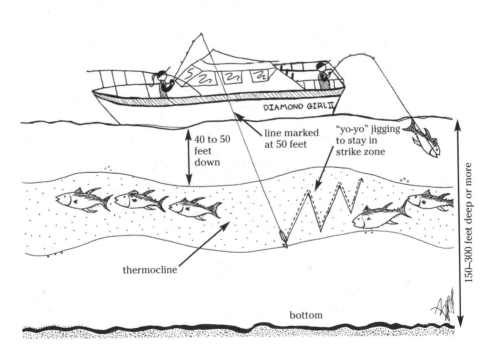

Diamond Jigging a Thermocline for Tuna

Thermoclines are one of your best bets for working diamond jigs for school tuna. Capt. Alex Malgieri hefts a bluefin he caught jigging in the thermocline off southern Massachusetts. *Photo by Capt. Ned Kittredge.*

A thermocline is a horizontal transition layer of seawater defined by temperature. A boundary exists between the underlying heavier and colder water and the lighter and warmer water above. Because water isn't perfectly transparent, most sunlight is absorbed in the surface layer, which warms as a result. Wind and waves churn the water in the upper layer and distribute heat within it. Below this layer the temperature drops rapidly.

In southern waters the thermocline may occur in depths up to 300 feet and last year round. In northern waters the thermocline appears in depths of about 40 feet and usually vanishes during the winter before resuming in late spring. The demarcation line deepens and becomes more distinguished as summer progresses.

You can find the thermocline by idling your boat (to reduce turbulence) and tuning a high-quality fishfinder or sonar to its highest frequency for maximum resolution. Slowly increase the gain until the thermocline appears on the screen. It should look like a pronounced horizontal line. The thermocline zone is rich with oxygen and light and, therefore, plankton. Plankton, in turn, draws baitfish, which then draw predators. The thermocline zone is the best area in which to jig for tuna.

Becoming familiar with these basic elements of oceanography will help you understand the reason for certain water conditions and how and where fish are attracted to specific areas. As you improve you knowledge of local hotspots, enhanced by keeping a fishing journal, you will see your catch rates improve.

II
Fishing Diamond Jigs

4

HOW TO RIG AND TUNE DIAMOND JIGS

"Tune" is my term for changing or adjusting the hardware, appearance or configuration of a jig to better suit the fishing conditions or targeted species. For optimal lure performance, however, the first place to start the tune-up isn't with the jig itself, but rather with your line choice, leader type and line-to-jig connections.

Some no-frills anglers, disregarding super braid line, load their reels with straight 40- or 50-pound monofilament and simply tie the heavy line directly to a heavy jig with a clinch knot. When aggressive predators like bluefish are abundant, and stiff currents or deep water aren't factors, this set-up is probably just as effective as more complex rigging, but when fish are located in deep, fast water or they are finicky or widely scattered, a more advanced approach to lines and rigging can significantly improve catch rates.

Super braids, sometimes called "super lines," have a smaller diameter than monofilament of the same pound test, which makes them less visible to fish. The narrow diameter allows anglers to load more line on their reels. A comparatively fuller spool also reduces the increased drag on a fish as the spool diameter shrinks during long runs or in deep water. Braids have almost no stretch, which instantly conveys strikes to the rod tip and allows for more positive hook sets. Super lines have advanced technologically since their introduction to the market a few years ago, making them rounder for less digging into spools under pressure, softer and more castable.

Braids are slippery in comparison to traditional monofilament, which makes snug knots difficult to tie, however, a Palomar is one of the easiest and best knots for attaching a swivel to braid without slippage under pressure. Experienced anglers often wind mono backing on their reels before loading braid to prevent the line from slipping around the spool. Using mono as backing also conserves the more expensive braided line and adds firmness to the spool to help reduce backlashes, especially when casting.

Mono is a nylon-based material born in 1938 when the DuPont company created a group of synthetic superpolymers called nylon. Monofilament has approximately 15-percent stretch under pressure, which is a disadvantage for most types of deep-water jigging, but mono is much less expensive than other specialty lines, and it has a following with offshore anglers who like its stretch to help reduce impacts from hard-hitting fish like tuna.

Anglers who want the best of both worlds in deep-water situations—cushioning stretch and increased sensitivity—first fill their spool with super braid because of its narrow diameter and less drag in strong currents, and then they top-shot the braid with 50 feet or more of mono for its shock-absorption qualities.

Leaders can be composed of fluorocarbon, monofilament or wire. Fluorocarbon is a polymer that's almost invisible underwater because it refracts sunlight at about the same rate as does water. Fluoro holds up well to deteriorative elements like sunshine, fuel, battery acid and even insect repellent. Unlike mono, fluoro doesn't absorb water so it won't weaken or stretch excessively like mono does when saturated, which also makes it more sensitive to subtle strikes in deep water.

Although you never need to fill your spool with it, fluorocarbon is a good leader choice when fish are in shallow, clear water or for those predators with sharp eyesight like tuna. Fluorocarbon is stiffer than mono, which is helpful in many leader applications, but knots are more difficult to tie perfectly in fluoro. When tying knots in fluoro, always wet the line to help cinch the knot down tight, and to reduce momentary heat build-up that weakens the connection. Monofilament is cheaper, easier to tie and is still the best all-purpose choice for deep, dark waters and for fish that aren't line shy.

Lengths for mono or fluoro leaders can range from 18 inches for casting small jigs, such as when targeting false albacore, to 4 to 6 feet or more when jigging over wrecks or in schools of competitive fish swiping at the lure. A wire leader, whether made of single or multiple strands, is seldom necessary because fish rarely engulf a jig deeply enough to reach the leader. When pursuing some fast and aggressive fish with sharp teeth like king mackerel, however, may require a short length of bite wire, usually 60- to 120-pound test, tied between the clear leader and the jig. I'll discuss more specifics on leader choices in the individual species chapters.

You can use one of three basic systems to connect a main line to a leader. The first connection is a line-to-line knot, like a double uni-knot or a blood knot, which allows you to reel a long leader into the rod guides. The second connection is a heavy-duty barrel swivel, which always remains on the main line. If you need to detach the rig for storage or transportation just snip the leader at the swivel and tie it on again next time. For convenience, and to prevent damage to the guides, the swivel should be large enough to prevent it from being reeled in through the rod tip. The third connection is tying the main line to a snap-swivel, necessitating a surgeon's loop knot in the leader to which you clip the snap. Each system has its advantages and disadvantages, and the final choice is personal preference.

The connection from main line to swivel, or leader to jig, can be as simple as the basic clinch knot mentioned earlier. To allow more fluttering action on your jigs, however, you can use a non-slip loop knot (in the case of using a snap-swivel connection, your leader would then have a loop on both ends), which won't restrict the jig's movement with thick leader material. Other good knots include the uniknot, Palomar and doubled improved clinch. For easy tying instructions, visit www.animatedknots.com.

Amateurs often use a snap or a snap-swivel to connect the main line or leader directly to the jig. This configuration is very common when purchasing pre-made wire leaders, most of which feature a small swivel on the line end and a snap on the terminal end. The snap-to-lure system does make lure changes quick and easy, but it also has several disadvantages:

First, snaps can rob the lure of its intended action, making it sluggish on the retrieve and restrict its fluttering action on the drop. Second, some fish are wary of snap-swivels, especially when attached to small lures intended for keen-eyed predators like bonito and false albacore. Third, and perhaps most important, any strong-jawed fish can clamp down on a snap-swivel and open it, causing the loss of fish and jig. For easy lure changes, use a Palomar knot to tie a snap-swivel to the main line. Tie a loop knot in the top end of the mono or fluorocarbon leader of each rigged diamond jig. That way, you can quickly switch out jigs or remove them for transportation while keeping the snap away from the lure's O-ring.

For the most beneficial tune-up to your jigs remove the factory-installed hook and replace it with one of a different style, size or strength. Diamond jigs are one of the simplest and deadliest lures ever created, but you really can build a better mousetrap by changing out the hook.

When preparing diamond jigs intended to fish on rugged bottoms or for toothy pelagics, remove any treble hook and replace it with a single. Treble hooks snag bottom more easily and make unhooking fish much more difficult and dangerous.

The standard, single diamond-jig hook is an O'Shaughnessy in size 7/0 or 8/0. Only use 7/0s for smaller fish like schoolie striped bass. The thinner gauge of the 7/0s straightens under excessive pressure of big fish, especially when lifting your trophy from the water by the jig. A hook with better penetrating and holding power is the Siwash, often used for salmon in the Northwest and bluefish in the Northeast.

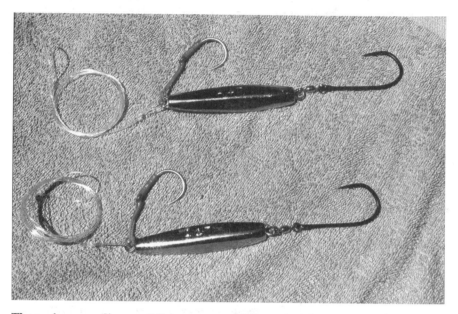

These 4-ounce diamond jigs were tuned by switching out the treble hooks and replacing them with single 7/0 Siwash hooks affixed to the swivel end. Dangling assist hooks increase the chance for catching fish like striped bass or school tuna. Four feet of 80-pound mono leader attached to the jig with a loop knot completes the rigging.

One of the best Siwash hooks on the market is Owner's new 7/0 and 8/0 Cutting-Point Stinger open-eye hook in black. The triple-edged cutting point easily penetrates tough jaws, and the 3X-strong shank and deep-throat gap handle large fish. The black finish sometimes fishes better than a shiny hook does because it's much less visible and gives the jig a 3-inch-overall shorter profile to help match small baitfish profiles.

I intentionally allow shiny hooks on my diamond jigs to rust by leaving them exposed to the weather year-round, but I do sharpen the points before each use. I've found that dark or rusty hooks get more strikes than shiny versions when fishing for predators keying on smaller baitfish. Because they're rough, rusty hooks also "grip" a fish's mouth better along the bend than do slick, new hooks. Use common sense, however, because excessive rusting weakens metal.

Treble hooks have their place when diamond jigging, especially when you're targeting species like tuna feeding in mid water and headed for the cooler. In this case, shiny treble hooks may produce more hits than dark hooks because their action resembles a baitfish's beating tail. Tuna pros like Capt. Ned Kittredge feel most jigs "right out of the box" need their treble hooks exchanged because those supplied are not suitable for tuna and similar powerful species. Kittredge removes the factory trebles and replaces them with a heavy-duty version; he favors those made by Owner.

The Owner 4X strong is one of the toughest treble hooks available. Many expert anglers consider it an automatic upgrade for almost any factory-rigged diamond-style jig. Its features include a short shank, Owner's famous super-sharp Power Points for quick penetration and a corrosion-resistant, vacuum-tinned finish. As with other fine manufacturers selling similar heavy-duty trebles, sizes that are typically available include every size from 4 through 5/0.

One of the strongest split rings for the hook-to-jig connections is the Owner Hyper Wire series. These are extra heavy-duty split rings are made from high-quality stainless steel with an instant "springback" feature after opening. Owner is one of the few companies that supplies pound-test ratings for its split rings, available in eight sizes from size 4 at a 50-pound test rating to size 11 at a 250-pound rating.

If you get into a situation with short strikes from high-speed pelagics like king mackerel, when they swipe at your diamond jig but miss it, Texas coast jigging expert and outdoor writer, Patrick Lemire, suggests removing the treble hook and creating a stinger configuration by adding a 3-inch length of wire between the hook and the jig. Attach the wire on both ends with haywire twists. It's important to camouflage the stinger by using coffee-colored wire and a dark treble hook (let your hooks rust over, buy black ones or spray them with flat black, green or blue paint designed for metal) so predators will not see the shiny hook-and-wire combo and still short-strike it. If you want to be rigged for a potential world-record catch, be sure to check out "IGFA Assist-Hook Rules" in Chapter 17.

Rigged stinger hooks are now available commercially. The Mustad hook company, for instance, sells a black-nickel 3X strong treble hook in sizes 1/0 and 3/0. It's rigged to a 90-pound-test, 1.9-inch, wire leader sporting a barrel swivel on the opposite end.

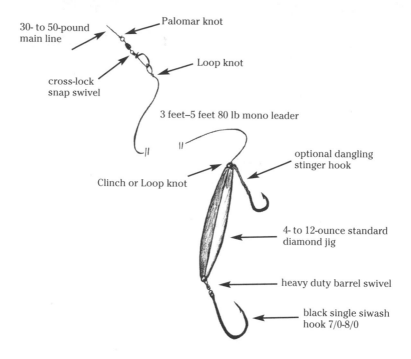

The following labels appear on the diagram:

30- to 50-pound main line

Palomar knot

Loop knot

cross-lock snap swivel

3 feet–5 feet 80 lb mono leader

optional dangling stinger hook

Clinch or Loop knot

4- to 12-ounce standard diamond jig

heavy duty barrel swivel

black single siwash hook 7/0-8/0

Example of Rigged Diamond Jig

The stinger rig is effective for casting to fish working near the surface. Using a high-quality spinning reel loaded with 30- to 50-pound braid attached to a 7- to 7½-foot medium-heavy to heavy spinning rod, cast the jig to the fish, slowing its velocity slightly so the rig straightens before hitting the water. Allow the jig to sink several feet and then retrieve it fast.

The latest styles of hooks include "dancing" or "assist" stinger hooks that dangle off the jig on short special leaders, and circle hooks. Both types can be used on diamond jigs. Although dangling hooks were originally designed for Butterfly-style jigs, they come pre-rigged to tethers and are sold separately from lures. Dancing hook sizes range from 1/0 to 9/0 and are intended to be rigged at the head end of the jig.

Attach dancing hooks to any jig by looping them through a split ring or solid O-ring connected between the leader and the lure's eye ring. They are beneficial for predators like striped bass that attack prey at the head rather than the tail, but you should consider removing the dangling hooks and replacing them with standard hooks rigged off the tail-end of the lure when toothy fish like bluefish move in. Otherwise, a head-rigged hook may place fish's dentistry too close to a nylon-type leader.

The other unlikely candidate for a tune-up hook on vertical jigs is a circle hook. Capt. Ricky Mola, owner of Fisherman's World tackle center in Norwalk, Connecticut, is credited as the first expert in the Northeast to experiment with circle hooks on diamond and Butterfly-style jigs. Mola noticed some bluefish and striped bass were getting deep-hooked in the throat or gills, which is a drawback of using J-hooks. This problem, which harms fish and makes catch-and-release difficult, isn't uncommon during feeding frenzies when fish are striking aggressively. Capt. Mola thought using circle hooks might reduce the injury rate, but they might also reduce the hook-up rate.

Much to Mola's surprise, as well as that of jigging expert George Poveromo of *George Poveromo's World of Saltwater Fishing* on ESPN 2 television, the catch rate not only didn't suffer—it improved! Over several days of trial fishing together, Mola and Poveromo experienced numerous hook-ups without any throat-hooked fish. Jumping blue-fish also failed to throw the circle hooks as they do J-hooks. Part of the hook-up trick, according to Poveromo, is squidding (10 turns of steady reeling followed by free spooling back to the bottom) the lure rather than jigging it yo-yo style, especially not allowing any slack in the line during the drop.

The other important technique when fishing with circle hooks is not reacting instantly to a strike by yanking up hard for a hook set. That motion only pulls the hook out of a fish's mouth before the point has a chance to penetrate in the jaw. Instead, just continue steady reeling through the hook set and into the fight.

Mola starts his jig tune-up by removing the hook(s) from a dia-mond- or Butterfly-style jig of 4 to 6 ounces. He then adds a 50- to 60-pound-test stainless split ring to the fixed ring on the tail end of the jig. To that he attaches a 75-pound-test barrel swivel and finally adds a 6/0 Gamakatsu offset circle hook to the other end of the swivel.

For larger predators you can also try attaching a circle hook fea-turing factory-rigged, stainless-steel welded rings or ball bearing swivels, such as Owner's ringed or ball-bearing-swiveled Super Mutu circle hooks, available in sizes 4/0 to 12/0, but these are more expensive.

You may need to experiment with the best circle hook size for your needs but a range of 6/0 to 8/0 is a good starting point. Although some experts favor Gamakatsu circle hooks and hardware, other top brands like Eagle Claw, Mustad and Owner are equally effective.

Another tune-up option for vertical jigs is a section of colorful plas-tic or rubber tubing pulled over the hook shank. This is a common dressing when jigging for cod, bluefish and striped bass. In situations like cod fishing, the tubing is intended to resemble a sand eel. In other applications, it may look like the tentacles on a fleeing squid (remember, squid swim "backwards"), but the tubing doesn't last long when catching fish with razor-sharp teeth. It also adds 3 to 4 inches to the overall length of the lure, which may be a disadvantage when local baitfish are small.

A few anglers dress their chrome diamond jigs by adding holographic decals, which may include eyes, patterns or bright colors to two or more sides. You can see an example of this on Deadly Dick lures.

Glow strips are another stick-on decal you can use, which will give your jig a "pulsing" look like a live squid or flashing baitfish in the depths. The self-stick glow material is available in 3-inch by 6-inch sheets, which you must cut to fit your lures. Most craft shops and tackle stores carry them.

Expert Patrick Lemire suggests a unique method of "charging" your glow strips with light the quickest way possible. Lemire uses a detachable flash unit designed for 35mm cameras—digital or film—but it must have a "test button." Hold the flash unit, which usually functions on four AA batteries, close to the glow strips and fire the flash. The light charge will be immediate, brighter and longer lasting than is otherwise achievable.

Although various decals may be effective when fish are picky, the stickers won't last too long when targeting toothy predators like bluefish. It's hard to beat a plain chrome jig.

On one charter-boat trip on the Atlantic I watched a customer carefully applying and buffing metal polish on his jigs to enhance their shine en route to the grounds. For experts and serious anglers, any small advantage seems worth the effort of tuning a jig.

5

BLUEFISH, STRIPED BASS AND WEAKFISH

Bluefish are a migratory, pelagic species distributed around the world in temperate coastal areas with the exception of the eastern Pacific. On the East Coast, they are found from Florida to Maine, where they migrate north in spring and south in autumn. Blues may reach 15 or more years of age and weigh up to 31 pounds, which is the current world record. However, a blue in the 18- to 25-pound range is considered very large and a true trophy.

Bluefish are unique eating machines consuming up to twice their weight in baitfish each day. The only member of the family Pomatomidac, *Pomatomus saltatrix* has a reputation for the hardest fight of any fish its size. A bluefish may bulldog into the depths, burn a drag across a sand flat or jump clear of the surface (*saltatrix* is Latin for "leaper") and shake its head hard enough to hurl a 4-ounce diamond jig back into a boat.

Nicknamed choppers and marine piranhas because of their razor-sharp teeth and snapping, vice-like jaws, bluefish often feed in large pods that viciously gorge on schools of hapless baitfish. When in an eating frenzy, these voracious and opportunistic feeders may bite anything in their path, including floating soda cans and their own young. On several occasions they have even attacked bathers. Unfortunately, bluefish's dentistry rules out the use of most bucktail and soft-plastic jigs because just one fish can destroy the body material. This same characteristic requires vigilance when unhooking bluefish to prevent lacerated fingers.

Bluefish feed through the entire water column and favor baitfish-like adult and juvenile menhaden, squid, herring and butterfish, which they often chase up from the depths and trap against the surface, creating spectacular surface blitzes. Unlike striped bass, bluefish attack from the rear, often biting larger prey in half tail-first. These feeding characteristics make blues prime targets for diamond jigging, which is the most productive way to catch them. Because di-

Bluefish are a prime target for jig fishermen. Robert Person landed this big blue with a Butterfly jig rigged with a single 7/0 Siwash hook attached to the jig's tail end with a split ring and barrel swivel. He removed the standard dangling assist hook in anticipation of toothy bluefish. Shimano's Butterfly jigging reel (Trinidad Narrow Special TN 16N with a 6.2:1 gear ratio) and parabolic rod (6'9" Trevala rated for 20- to 50-pound braid) complete the tackle package.

amond jigs are fast, shiny, "tooth proof" and rigged with a hook at the rear, it's impossible to find a more deadly and efficient bluefish lure.

The two most common locations for vertical jigging bluefish and striped bass are rips and open water around baitfish schools. Jigging in baitfish schools driven up by predators is "dialed in" target fishing because you know predators are present and actively feeding.

The same holds true at times along rips where you mark pockets of fish on your electronics or see them breaking on top. During these occasions, good results are a guarantee, but just because you don't see fish breaking in front of a rip line or mark them beneath your hull doesn't mean they're not present and feeding. This is when you blind or "saturation" jig, which means thoroughly covering an area and trying to draw fish in from the immediately surrounding waters.

Once you arrive at promising structure—easy to find by studying a local chart—motor uptide of the rip line while watching your depthfinder. Where the structure levels off to flat bottom, stop the boat and let the current start to pull you back toward the reef. Immediately drop your jig to the bottom, and work it by speed squidding until your boat reaches the crest of the reef or the rip line. At that point, reel in your jig and run back upcurrent to make additional passes, using electronics, triangulation or a retrievable marker buoy, such as an empty bleach bottle attached to a brick with an appropriate length of twine, to repeat successful drifts.

"Squidding" is the most productive technique for bluefish holding in front of rips. Free-spool your jig until it hits bottom, then immediately engage your reel, retrieve the jig 10 quick turns, drop it back down and hit bottom again. Repeat this procedure in rapid succession throughout each drift. If a pass proves unproductive, saturation fish the rip by trying different starting points along the reef until you find blues.

Capt. Al Anderson of the charter boat *Prowler* out of Snug Harbor, Rhode Island, uses a slightly different squidding technique, which is very useful when bluefish disperse throughout the water column, such as over a bottom contour with significant vertical relief or when fishing open water under breaking baitfish schools.

When squidding for bluefish using his system, the angler hits bottom with the jig then uses a steady retrieve all the way to the surface rather than just taking 10 turns up. Using a moderate reeling speed can reduce chances for cutoffs from bluefish swiping at the lure throughout the water column. Avoid yo-yo jigging (lifting the jig and then allowing it to tumble by using long rod tip sweeps) because it may cause bluefish to miss the lure and cut the line, and should be avoided.

Squidding is also effective for bluefish working bait schools in harbors or migrating over a flat bottom. Most anglers see fish breaking on top and start slinging plugs at them. Spin casting is fun but not always very productive. The baitfish are busting because predators are driving them up from the depths and trapping them against the surface. While it's exciting to watch a big blue crash a plug, if your goal is a high catch-rate, diamond jigging will outfish plugging by a considerable margin, if only because bluefish blitzes are like icebergs— 90 percent of their mass is underwater.

When you spot a blitz or working birds, position your boat just ahead of the action and turn off the motor. Don't plow into the school because you'll spook the fish and drive them down, which will also anger nearby fishermen. Let the wind or current carry you into the activity while squidding a jig beneath the surface frenzy.

Four-ounce diamonds are the ideal size for inshore waters like Long Island Sound, Buzzards Bay or Chesapeake Bay. However, for the big rips like the Race at the mouth of Long Island Sound, the Montauk rips and the rips off Cape Cod, you may need jigs as heavy as 8 to 12 ounces. Use the lightest weight possible for the conditions.

When rigging for bluefish, tie 36 to 40 inches of 40- to 80-pound mono abrasion leader to the jig. That handles the blue on the hook as well as protecting against free-swimming "buddy" fish that graze the leader while swiping at the lure in the hooked fish's mouth. While some fishermen use wire leaders attached to their bluefish rigs, my experience suggests that this produces fewer strikes than a mono leader, which is durable enough for bluefish when jigging.

Always switch out factory-rigged treble hooks with 8/0 O'Shaughnessy or Siwash singles to make unhooking simpler and safer for you and the fish. Single hooks also greatly reduce the chances of hanging bottom on rough structure. If you want to experience some really fun bluefishing with easier releases, try filing or crimping the barb down.

Fish 4- to 6-ounce diamonds with medium- to medium-heavy action, fast taper, 6½-foot boat rods rated for 20- to 40-pound line matched with a medium conventional level-wind reel like a Penn 310 GTi or Shimano Tekota 500. Fill your spool over halfway with backing like 30-pound Dacron or mono and top-shot it to capacity with 30-pound super braid. If cost for braid is a factor, 20- to 25-pound mono will also work, but when your line is whacked and parted by another bluefish, you'll wish you had the tougher super braid. After all, just one saved lure makes up the cost difference. Line drag is also significantly reduced by using braid, which is important for helping to maintain vertical drops in rips.

If you choose to go with lighter gear for greater sport, you can tie on 24 inches of 60-pound mono leader and connect it to the main line with a No. 8, 50-pound-test swivel. Use reels like Penn International 965 and 975 baitcasters spooled with 15-pound line matched with 7-foot, medium-action rods.

Anglers plying deep-water reefs or shoals of 150 to 200 feet deep with swift currents must often use 8- to 16-ounce jigs with 50-pound super braid to hold near bottom. When fishing big rips, use tackle beefy enough to crank a heavy bluefish or bass to the surface before your craft drifts stern-first into a cresting rip line. This requires heavy-action rods matched with bigger reels like a Penn 3/0 or 4/0 Special Senator, Penn 320 or 330 GTi or Shimano Tekota 700, which will handle the heavier jigs as well as the rugged conditions and provide faster cranking speed.

Anglers commonly catch stripers, and sometimes weakfish, in the same waters as bluefish and, having similar feeding habits, they are often caught at the same time with the same gear. Therefore, the techniques and tackle are similar for all three, but pros alter their methods when targeting bass.

Striped bass are the most popular and valuable sportfish in the Northeast and Mid Atlantic regions and rank very high as a favorite target nationally. Bass live primarily inshore but are sometimes caught in offshore shoal waters such as Stellwagen Bank in the Gulf of Maine. They prefer rocky, current-swept habitats like boulder fields, hence the nickname "rockfish" (not to be confused with the Pacific species called rockfish, although transplanted striped bass are also found along the West Coast). Stripers are anadromous, meaning they live in saltwater but spawn in rivers. Contrary to what many people believe they are not a true member of the sea bass family.

According to Capt. Al Anderson, the world leader in tagged-and-released striped bass in the American Littoral Society tag program, New England's large stripers spend their winters from New York to Virginia. These fish spawn in rivers emptying into the Chesapeake Bay, as well as in the Delaware and Hudson rivers.

Stripers sometimes rest and feed behind current-swept structure, but most often they hold in the sweet spot in front of the reef as do bluefish. Bass prowl in this quiet water where their energy expenditure is minimized as they wait for baitfish to swim past. Because they're efficient feeders and conserve calories whenever possible, stripers hang much closer to the protection of structure than do bluefish.

Many reefs hold stripers at the end of the structure, rather than along their mid section, and some reefs gain or lose fish as current direction and velocity changes during the course of a tide. Vertical strike zones are typically small, so work your jig close to the bottom where stripers are holding stationary in the current, always returning to the precise location of a productive pass.

Squidding for stripers is an effective way to catch them with vertical jigs. After running uptide of a rip line to where the flattest contour is, quickly free-spool your jig until it bumps bottom. Bass often hit jigs on the way down, so the drop is as important as the retrieve.

Maintain a vertical line whenever you can. If your line becomes too diagonal, reel your jig to the surface and start a new drop. Diagonal drops are especially problematic when the tide and wind oppose each other, because the wind holds the boat back against the current rather than allowing it to keep pace with your tide-swept lure. Diagonal drops aren't as productive because they restrict the fluttering action of the jig as it falls toward the bottom due to increased line drag.

Once the diamond hits bottom, immediately engage the reel and start your retrieve—a curious striper following the jig down loses interest and darts away if the lure sits for more than a couple seconds. Take about ten moderate-speed turns up, but not as fast as when squidding for bluefish. Repeat the process until you've cleared the hump of the reef but, unlike bluefishing, continue working down the backside of the reef into deeper water. If you don't have a depthfinder, this means drifting well into the rip. But don't risk your vessel's safety if the rip is too rough, especially if floating in stern-first.

One way to refine bluefish-style squidding and to better target bass is by slowing your retrieve and initially taking about five turns off the bottom. Pause for a moment and then take another four or five turns before free-spooling the jig back down. This stop-and-go movement sometimes triggers an instinctive strike.

Another popular vertical-jigging technique for stripers is the yo-yo method, which experts don't recommend for bluefish. If blues are mixed with stripers, as they often are, it's better to use the squidding technique described above. The yo-yo method entails dropping your lure to the bottom, engaging the reel and then taking a 4- to 5-foot upward sweep of the rod at moderate speed. Immediately drop the rod tip with enough speed to create slack line as the jig falls. No reeling is involved. Most bass strikes come on the drop, but anglers who don't provide enough slack for their lures to flutter on the fall receive fewer strikes.

Traditional diamond jigs, as well as weighted jigging spoons like Luhr-Jensen's Krocodile and Crippled Herring in the 3- to 5-ounce range are good choices for stripers. Generally, the smaller the jig the

Larisa DeSantis landed this striped bass using a standard 4-ounce diamond jig rigged with a single 8/0 O'Shaughnessy hook attached via a barrel swivel. The jig's tail-end O-ring is mashed flat from striking reefs in Long Island Sound. Three feet of 80-pound mono leader attached with a loop knot completes the rigging.

better its action and the more closely it matches local baitfish, including herring, butterfish, small menhaden, squid, sand eels and shad, which are all favorite bass forage. Three-to 5-ounce jigs are the perfect all-around choice for bass because they are small enough to resemble the prey, flutter well on the drop and are heavy enough to easily reach bottom in waters up to 100 feet deep.

The new brand of Japanese flutter-style jigs, including Shimano's Lucanus jig, are excellent for striped bass, rigged with the dancing hook on an O-ring between the jig and the leader. Another new spin on hook rigging is to remove the factory-installed tail hook (treble or single) and replace it with an 8/0 circle hook. According to reports by Capt. Ricky Mola, a striper expert and fishing innovator from Norwalk, CT, circle hooks perform well on bass jigs, grabbing and holding better than do standard hooks.

Buy single-hook models whenever possible. Treble hooks, while more effective at hooking and retaining fish, are also more damaging to the bass. They're also more likely to snag bottom, difficult to unhook and dangerous in a pitching craft. If your jigs have trebles, switch them over to singles.

When targeting stripers, I carry jigs rigged with 7/0 and 8/0 single hooks. If the bass are schoolies of up to, say, 28 inches, I go with the 7/0s for a better catch rate, but if large linesiders and big bluefish are on the reefs, I fish strictly with size 8/0s. The thinner-gauged 7/0s straighten with the pressure of bigger fish, especially if you lift them into the boat by grabbing the jig. Big stripers (as well as bluefish and weakfish) have large mouths; therefore, using larger hooks is never an issue.

For leader material, tie on 3 feet of 50- to 80-pound fluorocarbon and use a non-slip loop knot to allow the jig more action. Although schoolie bass don't require such a heavy leader, it doesn't deter them, and you'll be glad to have it when big, toothy bluefish start slashing at the lure or a cow bass drags the line over some rocks or around a lobster trap rope. Never use wire leaders because they hinder a jig's motion and turn away cautious stripers.

Rod and reels for bass are similar to those for bluefish. However, for yo-yo type jigging, some fishermen prefer to use longer rods, such as 7-footers, for longer sweeps.

Weakfish

If you've never had the pleasure of waging wits with weakfish, think of them as a cross between bluefish and stripers. Unlike bluefish, they

Large weakfish eagerly strike diamond jigs, especially when rigged with a tube over the hook. Because weakfish numbers are low they are often an unexpected bonus while targeting striped bass and bluefish.

are not built for sustained, open-water attacks on baitfish pods; for example, you'll never see a school of them blitzing bait a half-mile off the beach, but similar to stripers they hold near to the shore and favor structure where they can ambush prey. They are less fussy than bass and are attracted to big, bright jigs just like bluefish.

Weakfish, like stripers, have a varied diet consisting of the predominant forage found in their holding areas. Weakies adapt well to local conditions, and although usually found near the bottom they will feed at any depth depending on the food source. Large weakfish frequent beaches, but when the water gets warm they usually retreat to nearshore reefs and ledges where they gobble squid, butterfish, adult menhaden and herring.

Depending on where you fish, there may be one wave of migrating fish or two distinct pulses. Usually the smaller fish follow the larger ones. In southern New England, shoreline weakfishing begins in May and lasts through June. In the mid Atlantic, however, the action may start along the beaches in April. During the dog days of July and August, the reefs and rips become your best bet for hooking a bruiser. A fall migration usually produces a flurry in September; unfortunately, the population in the Northeast hasn't been strong enough recently to support an extensive autumn fishery.

Weakfish are usually so scattered that they are difficult to target directly when diamond or bucktail jigging. Lucky anglers usually catch them as a bonus when they least expect one. Therefore, use the same jigging tackle and methods you would for bluefish and stripers and just hope you are one of the fortunate anglers who catch a big weakfish in a rip during the summer.

When fighting a big weakfish (called a "weak" fish not due to lack of strength but because of their papery thin mouth), always keep your line tight so the fish can't use head shakes to easily tear out the hook.

6

FALSE ALBACORE, BONITO
AND MACKEREL

False albacore and bonito were once considered trash species in the Northeast and Mid-Atlantic regions. Now, aficionados call these highly-prized light-tackle gamefish "exotics," and they command much attention from East Coast fishermen. Sometimes incorrectly categorized together as "bonito," novice anglers often have trouble distinguishing them apart.

False albacore, technically named little tunny (*Euthynnus alletteratus*), are also called Fat Albert, little tuna, bloody mackerel, albie and apple knockers (the latter of which because they appear in southern New England when the apples are ripening and falling), and in Florida they're called bonito. Albies have a more tuna-like football shape than bonito and feature distinctive vermiculated markings along their backs. They have no scales except around the pectoral fin and lateral line and possess only tiny teeth. Albies have a scattering of dark spots between the pectoral and ventral fins, and their two dorsal fins are separated by a space. The first dorsal is tall and spike-shaped.

False albacore are generally bigger, stronger, more abundant and easier to catch than bonito. They average up to 25 inches in length and usually run less than 15 pounds with anything larger considered a trophy. The all-tackle world record is just over 35 pounds. Their flesh is dark, oily, strong and of poor eating quality; therefore, you should release them. Albies live for 10 to 15 years, about the same as bluefish, but about half that of striped bass.

Atlantic Bonito (*Sarda sarda*) are also called bonito, common bonito, green bonito, katonkel and bones, and they are not the same fish Florida anglers call bonito or oceanic bonito, which are actually little tunny or false albacore. Green bonito have a narrower body and a smaller, more sloping dorsal fin than do false albacore; no space exists between the first and second dorsal fin. Bones are distinguished by straight tiger stripes running their body length above the lateral line, thus avoiding confusion with skipjack tuna (oceanic bonito,

Dan Martinez shows off his first false albacore, which he landed on a small diamond jig cast to a pod of breaking fish in the eastern end of Long Island Sound. It's important to use fluorocarbon leader for these sharp-eyed predators.

Katsuwonus pelamis), which have dark, horizontal stripes running along the abdomen. Freshly caught bones also show faint, wide vertical bars across their sides. Bonito have large, sharp, pointed teeth, an entirely scaled body and a curved lateral line. The average fish weighs 4 to 10 pounds with the all-tackle record topping 18 pounds. Bonito have much lighter flesh than false albacore and are good eating, especially grilled or as sushi.

This large bonito fell for Jerry Martin's diamond jig worked under a school south of Rhode Island. Unlike false albacore, bonito are excellent eating either grilled or as sushi.

Occasionally mixing with false albacore and bonito are Spanish mackerel (*Scomberomorus maculatus*). Spanish mackerel, nicknamed "Spanish," are more slender than albies and bonito. Spanish resemble both the king mackerel and cero mackerel but not the Atlantic mackerel. Spanish mackerel show golden spots across their bodies without stripes, easily distinguishing them from the tunas and Atlantic mackerel. Spanish average 18 to 24 inches and only 2 to 3 pounds. The all-tackle world record is 13 pounds. They are a good eating, but are the least common of the three exotics in northern waters.

Finding albies and bones (and Spanish mackerel if you're very lucky) is challenging; hooking and landing them is even more difficult. This is a light-tackle sport pursuing smart, high-speed fish with keen eyesight. Hunting them entails cruising likely stretches of coastline, usually along the uptide side of large rips or within a half mile of shorelines and estuary entrances, searching for breaking fish and/or working birds.

One challenge for anglers new to chasing these little tunas is distinguishing their surface action from that of bluefish. Bluefish tend to stay up longer, rise vertically and create "circular" splashes. False albacore and bonito feed in fast undulating patterns and make diagonal or slashing breaks. These scombroids (tuna family members) briefly trap and work bait against the surface, vanish and then seemingly pop up in an instant 50 or more yards away. Bluefish usually resurface in the same vicinity where they last surfaced.

The reason albies and bones can swim up and down through the water column so quickly is because they lack swim bladders. A swim bladder, located at the top of the abdominal cavity and under the backbone, is an internal gas balloon allowing fish to create neutral buoyancy and suspend at any depth. Tunas like false albacore and bonito must remain swimming at all times or they will sink because these predators don't have to adjust a bladder when changing depth. They can swim vertically down to the depths and diagonally at a much faster rate than other most other fish.

Once you locate a pod of bonito and/or false albies, the most common fishing technique is to quickly motor to the school and make a fast cast or two before the pod moves or settles. This method is known as the "run-and-gun." At times you'll keep your boat up on a plane just to stay with a fast-feeding cluster, which can top 25 mph swimming and approximately 40 mph when jumping. The run-and-gun is most successful with larger schools that remain in one spot for more than a few minutes. Sometimes you must chase around small pods for 15 minutes to a half hour before being able to hit them with a cast—and even then they don't always bite.

When possible, try approaching upcurrent or upwind and off to one side of a school. Position the boat parallel to the fish so everyone onboard can cast to it. Most captains kill their engine and let the boat drift into casting range. At times albies and bones are extremely boat shy, but when they're feeding heavily almost nothing bothers them and they may pop up right next to your craft.

Another method, the drift technique, involves cruising into an area of promising action, ideally where several pods are working, and then simply cutting the motor and waiting. The idea is to let a randomly moving school show within casting range. While you're waiting it's a good idea to blind cast around the boat, which often results in unexpected hits, but haul your line in fast and sight cast the moment fish surface nearby. When targeting a moving school, cast in front of the fish, leading them as a quarterback would a receiver running down field.

A third technique is trolling. After locating an area of breaking fish, you can troll two to four lines behind the boat at speeds between four and seven knots. Set the lures from 50 to 150 feet astern, although sometimes little tunas will surface directly in the prop wash to grab a lure.

Trolling is difficult if weeds clutter the surface. In that case, try casting around the weed lines or other floating debris. Albies and bones hold along weed patches when feeding on baitfish attracted by the cover.

The best trolling lures are 1- to 2-ounce bullet-head bucktails, skirted jigs, diamond jigs or other small metal jigs that won't spin when fast-trolled.

False albacore, bonito and Spanish mackerel forage on oily bait-fish including juvenile butterfish, silversides, sand eels, bay anchovies and baby bunker. Therefore, almost any small (½- to 1½-ounce) metal jig resembling a tiny baitfish may produce blazing strikes.

The best jigs for small tunas are those designed for both vertical jigging and casting. Hopkins Jigs, Swedish Pimples, Crippled Herring, Atom Shag-N-Shad jigs, Deadly Dicks and diamond jigs are among the favorites with albie and bonito pros.

After casting to a school, try rapidly reeling your jig so it runs just under the surface. If that technique fails to draw strikes try a stop-and-go retrieve, combined with rod-tip twitches, so the lure tumbles and flutters like an injured baitfish.

If lures fished alone still seem too large and don't draw strikes try adding a dropper fly 18 inches ahead of your jig. Popular flies include sparsely tied Clousers, Deceivers, Bunnies and various epoxy min-now patterns. Productive sizes are 2 to 3½ inches long and tied on 2/0 and smaller saltwater hooks. When using a fly for bonito, keep the tail material short; while albies inhale their food on a roll, bones use their sharp teeth to "nip" and may just grab the hair or feathers.

Use a high-capacity reel with a good drag system filled with approximately 12-pound mono or 15-pound super braid. Match the reel to a 7- to 7½-foot, medium/light graphite rod. For leader material, tie on 18 inches of 15- to 20-pound fluorocarbon with a uni-knot.

Some anglers try to be "sporting" by using line in the 4- to 8-pound range for bones and albies. This is a mistake because extra-light line necessitates long fights that produce low survival rates after release. Use the highest pound-test line and leader that is effective, bring fish to the boat as quickly as feasible and release them. Scombroids push water over their gills when swimming, rather than inhaling it as other fish can. Thus, spent or tired fish require a forceful jump start when released. Hold little tunas by the tail several feet above the surface and thrust them headfirst into the water to force oxygenated water over their gills.

7

SCHOOL TUNA

Small and medium school tuna love to hit diamond jigs. Jigging is one of the most fun and effective offshore methods of catching these large members of the mackerel family. Bluefin tuna are the most receptive to jigs, followed by green bonito, false albacore, true albacore (longfin) and yellowfin. Anglers do catch other types of tuna by jigging, but not as often. Two of the most popular ways to fish diamonds for tuna are accomplished concurrently while trolling or baitfishing.

One of the leading tuna experts and author of the book, *To Catch a Tuna*, is Capt. Al Anderson who has caught hundreds of school tuna offshore with small diamond jigs, and he recommends the following methods.

While trolling for school tuna, often in the vicinity of temperature breaks keep several suitable outfits rigged and ready for jigging action. When multiple bites occur on the trolled lines, indicating a school, pull back the throttles to idle speed and fight the tunas as usual. Boat all the fish except the last one, and instruct that angler to keep his tuna deep in the water but near the transom. Other members of the school, sometimes called buddy fish, tend to stay with the hooked fish, sometimes even swiping at the lure dangling from its mouth. Those are your diamond-jigging targets.

Turn your boat hard to one side and instruct another angler to pitch a jig forward toward the bow on the inward-turn side of the boat. As soon as the jig hits the water, the angler free spools the reel and allows his jig to sink to about 50 feet deep and then engages the reel. It's a good idea to pre-mark the main line by measuring 50 feet from the lure and tying on a series of tight half-hitches with waxed dental floss (the wax on the floss adds friction and reduces sliding). As the line comes tight from the boat's forward motion the jig will rise to about 40 feet where the angler should work it with a gentle yo-yo jigging motion.

When a tuna strikes the diamond jig, boat the original decoy fish, which is still in the water and probably spent, and use the new fish as the next decoy. Another angler should now lob another jig forward to hook a second buddy fish, and the process starts again. If done properly, it's possible to have continuous action with a series of fish before the school departs.

A good lure choice for school tuna is a 3- to 4-ounce Bridgeport-style diamond jig tied directly to a 30- to 50-pound-test mono main line. You can rig a 2- to 3-ounce jig on 30-pound mono for false albacore and bonito, a 4- to 6-ounce jig on 50-pound mono for school bluefin and small yellowfin and a 8-ounce jig on 100-pound mono for medium and even large tuna.

Regardless of lure size, it's important to purchase high-quality jigs for tuna because the wire end-loops and swivels must be as strong as possible. Premium jigs also have better chrome plating, which are more reflective and therefore often more enticing.

Another tuna jigging opportunity occurs from a boat drifting or at anchor when using chum and fresh whole or chunk baits, often in areas where draggers are working and discarding their bycatch, which acts like a huge chum line. Capt. Ned Kittredge, owner of the charterboat *Watch Out* from Westport, Massachusetts, is an expert who often fishes around trawlers and endorses these techniques.

Once you arrive in one of these areas you'll often mark school tuna feeding beneath your boat, usually at depths of 35 to 50 feet, which is in or near the thermocline. When you mark the thermocline or tuna at a certain depth you should measure off line from the tip of your jigging rod until you reach the corresponding distance. Then mark the line with several half-hitch wraps of rigging twine or waxed dental floss. Free spool a small jig to that depth and fish it there. You can experiment and fine tune the depth by leaving the mark in the water, at the rod tip or on the reel.

Engage the reel and perform a simple yo-yo jigging motion rather than speed-squidding as you would for bluefish. This action keeps your lure constantly in the strike zone. When the jig is fished properly, tuna usually strike as it settles, so it's critical to drop the rod tip quickly on each jigging cycle. That motion provides instant slack and allows the jig to fall horizontally and flutter to simulate a dying baitfish. This is an excellent application for the new deep-drop and flutter-style jigs such as a 3-ounce Spro Sushi Spoon or a 5-ounce Tormenter Chubby Jr.

Lowering the rod tip too slowly keeps light tension on the head of the jig and causes it to plummet vertically, thereby eliminating the enticing fluttering action. Be sure to watch for loops of line falling over your rod tip during the sudden rod-drop motion. If a line hang-

A wide variety of metal jigs, including Bridgeport Diamond Jigs, Crippled Herring and Yo-Zuri Metallic Sardines work well when fished behind a trolling boat or along a thermocline. Heavy-duty treble hooks and split rings are a good choice when tuning jigs for tuna. *Photo by Capt. Ned Kittredge.*

up occurs when a tuna hits the jig your line will part or your rod will fly overboard.

Three- to 4-ounce Bridgeport (or similar) diamond jigs are also an excellent choice, but first remove any factory-rigged hooks on the fixed-eye end of the jig. Replace them with an extra-strong 2/0 open-eye treble on the jig's swivel end by using a heavy-duty split ring.

A treble hook provides better odds of a hookup on a falling jig, and the swivel helps prevent tuna from leveraging against the lure's weight and wrenching out the hook. If you prefer single hooks, affix a Siwash open-eye size 4/0 to the swivel end. Unlike most other vertical jigging situations, the risk of snagging bottom with a treble hook doesn't apply here because tuna are pelagic (oceanic/mid-water) species.

For small school bluefin tuna, select 2/0 or 3/0 conventional reels with quality drags spooled with 30-pound mono, which is preferable to braided line because of the stretch needed for tuna impacts. Use about 5 feet of the heaviest leader possible, starting with 50-pound fluorocarbon, but dropping as low as 20-pound on bright days with small, fussy fish. Attach your leader to the main line with a blood knot and simply deal with any line twist rather than using an inline swivel for the connection, which may affect presentation or become caught in the guides.

All expert tuna anglers prefer lighter outfits for dedicated jigging rods simply because it's impossible to yo-yo jig heavy tackle for very long. Small, sturdy reels and light rods are a key to success, but some of these reels have limited line capacity. One way to solve this problem is to load your reels with thinner super braid and then tie on a top-shot of about 50 to 100 yards of monofilament, just the opposite of what you would do for deepwater bluefish or striped bass. Mono has much more shock-absorption quality than braid and is easier to untangle when lines cross while deep jigging. By the time a tuna pulls line out to the braid backing, tangles with other anglers usually aren't an issue because the fish is so far from the boat.

When selecting a spot to start jigging for tuna in the vicinity of trawlers, look for areas with breaking fish but also watch your electronics for deep-feeding tunas near the thermocline. Small bluefin often occur in waters of 30 fathoms or greater, so concentrate on the deeper edges of places like the Northeast's famous Mud Hole, located about 25 miles southeast of Rhode Island. Of course, you can find similar types of locations throughout the eastern seaboard. Once you choose a hot-looking location, cut your power—but never anchor when in the presence of constantly circling draggers—and then start

Albert Buchman jigged up this school bluefin tuna aboard the *Watch Out* when fishing among trawlers working the famous Mud Hole south of Massachusetts.

chumming with inch-wide baitfish pieces. Butterfish, whiting, mackerel, menhaden and herring all work well for chum.

Fishing in a crowded area means you're competing with other boats. Releasing a larger amount of cut bait around your boat will help keep the tuna in your chum slick. Never stop the chumming. A common mistake, particularly on smaller boats with only two or three anglers aboard, is to concentrate on hooked fish and neglect the chumming duties. Regardless of the number of anglers aboard or the battles occurring, you must maintain a continuous chum slick or risk losing your pod of fish to another nearby boat.

When you see tuna breaking on top, casting into the fray with a heavy-duty spinning outfit and small diamond jig or jigging lure like a Hopkins Shorty, Deadly Dick, Crippled Herring or Metallic Sardine is an effective and exciting method of catching school fish. Marking tuna beneath your hull when drifting over structure is another excellent application for jigging. On these occasions, results are almost a sure bet.

Just because you don't see fish breaking on top or aren't marking them beneath your hull doesn't mean they're not present and feeding in likely staging areas such as around bait on Stellwagen Bank in the Gulf of Maine. This is when you and your fellow anglers can blind or saturation jig, which means thoroughly covering an area and trying to draw fish in from the immediately surrounding waters.

In these instances, work your jig blind through the entire water column. Tuna will strike a jig at all depths over a bank, including right at the seafloor. As a bonus, you'll often pick up prize bottomfish like cod, pollock, haddock and, on rare occasions, even a halibut. This system is particularly effective with the new flutter-style jigs.

There are many different techniques, tackle types and heavy metal lures used around the country for jigging tuna, so it's important to research the favorite local methods and use them to your advantage. For example, in some areas where anchoring and bait chunking is popular, waters can be 150 feet or more and have a strong current, thereby requiring 8- and 10-ounce diamond jigs, but it's impractical to try to cover all locations, situations and variations here.

8

COD, HADDOCK AND POLLOCK

During most of the year, cod (as well as secondary targets pollock and haddock) feed omnivorously, but their primary forage base includes sand eels, herring, mackerel, whiting and squid. The two primary methods for simulating these prey species are bait fishing and diamond jigging.

Although bait fishing is productive and has its dedicated users, bait often draws spiny dogfish (large sand sharks), frequently in numbers too thick to fish through. That makes diamond and Norwegian-style cod jigs the top choice for many Northeast groundfish anglers, however, the most recent hot cod lures to hit the market are the new breed of Japanese-style deep-drop and flutter jigs, which may offer some advantages over standard jigs, but are more expensive.

The largest cod jigs of 24, 32 and even 43 ounces are the heaviest of the diamond-jig-style lures and are needed because of the strong currents found in the Northeast and the great depths cod inhabit. As always, however, you should still use the lightest jig possible for the conditions, thereby allowing the most action and natural presentation.

Experienced fishermen can impart action similar to a Norwegian jig to a standard diamond jig, and true diamonds produce equally well in many circumstances. In fact, some fishermen feel that diamond jigs are more efficient in greater depths because lacking the curved base, they can drop straighter and faster when properly fished.

Manufacturers traditionally produce Norwegian-style jigs with a large treble hook attached by a large, heavy-duty swivel. A short piece of red plastic tube adorns the hook shaft. Fishermen rig the Norwegian jig several ways, including as is, with a piece of bait on the treble hook, with a soft plastic teaser above the lure or they replace the treble hook with a single hook.

Probably the most effective way to catch cod involves diamond jigging with a soft-plastic teaser tied above the lure. Capt. Ned Kittredge

Large cod in the Gulf of Maine love a diamond jig rigged with a Bead Chain swivel and soft-plastic teaser over the hook.

and Capt. Al Anderson are among the experts who modify their diamond and Norwegian jigs. They do this by removing factory-rigged
hooks—especially treble hooks—and attaching a stainless-steel split
ring followed by a Bead Chain swivel and a single 9/0 Mustad or 10/0
Limerick hook.

Dress single hooks with a piece of red latex tubing long enough to
extend a few inches past the bend. Tubing resembles a sand eel, one
of the cod's primary foods. The Bead Chain swivel allows the hook
and tube to spin freely and enticingly when retrieved.

Cod anglers are divided on the subject of fishing with treble hooks
on their jigs. There's no doubt that trebles increase the hook-up rate,
and some fishermen feel that the work is so hard when plying great
depths with heavy lures that they need every advantage possible, but
treble hooks also cause a larger percentage of foul-hooked fish and,
as a result, fewer make it into the boat. Treble hooks also have a far
better chance of hanging on rough bottoms, wrecks or lobster gear,
and they make it harder to unhook and release short, undersize fish.
Treble hooks are preferable in waters of 200 feet or more, with a sand
or gravel bottom and holding primarily keeper-size fish. In shallower
water with short fish mixed in and when fishing over rough bottom,
wrecks or around lobster gear, a single hook is a better choice.

Whether you prefer single or treble hooks on your cod lures, you
should attach all hooks to a heavy-duty swivel rather than directly
to the base of the jig or via only a split ring. Cod spiral and twist as
you crank them to the surface, and these movements allow big fish to
leverage the hook against the weight of a heavy jig and wrench it from
their mouth. A swivel connection lets the fish spin independently of
the lure and prevents the hook from tearing out.

Using 80-pound mono leader, tie a blood knot 18 to 24 inches above
an appropriate-size diamond jig, leaving long tag ends for attaching
the teaser. Clip off one tag end close to the knot. On the other tag
end, about 6 inches long, clinch on a soft-plastic sand-eel teaser like
a Red Gill, Delta Eel or Felmlee Eel, rigged on a sharp 6/0 hook.

Pros recommend blood knots rather than three-way swivels because hardware can foul the dropper lures and impair a teaser's presentation. Finish your rig by clinching a large barrel swivel between
the main line and leader. Blood knots are ideal for this application because the tag ends standout perpendicularly to the main leader,
rather than parallel to it, thus helping to hold the teaser off the line.

One of most popular methods of working a cod jig is with an up-
and-down or yo-yo action. To yo-yo a diamond jig, free-spool your
lure to the bottom, take a couple of turns to clear any hangs, then lift

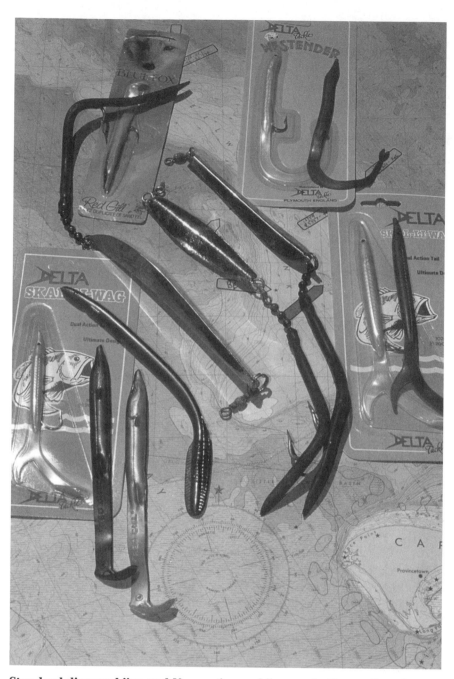

Standard diamond jigs and Norwegian cod jigs are both excellent lures for cod, pollock and haddock. Experts rig a Bead Chain swivel and soft-plastic teaser to the jig to simulate baitfish such as sand eels. *Photo by Capt. Ned Kittredge.*

the rod tip with brisk, snapping motions. Cod frequently strike on the down swing when the lure flutters toward the bottom, so be prepared to set the hook on the slightest bump.

Slow-speed squidding is another refined groundfish technique. It involves free-spooling the lure to the bottom, taking about 10 very slow turns up and repeating the process. This action allows the teaser and jig's tube to swim seductively and will often prompt lazy cod to strike at the spinning sand-eel imitation. With this system, the jig functions primarily as an attracting weight, not as the main enticement.

Inexperienced anglers, particularly aboard a party boat, start each drop by lowering their rig straight down into the water and often too slowly. You'll see many pros, however, cast or lob their jig either downwind (when drifting) or uptide (when anchored) and free-spool it as fast as possible. In other words, they either cast in the direction the boat is drifting or, if anchored, in the direction from which the tide is running. There's a good reason for it.

Even a short cast of 20 feet will help the jig drop to the bottom faster and stay in the strike zone longer while decreasing the time spent reeling in at drift's end. By casting downwind the lure should reach the bottom about when the boat and angler are over the same spot, thus the line is then running straight down rather than diagonally away and under the boat. When beginners use a straight drop, especially a slow one, the current and/or drift forces the jig to fall away from the angler rather than ending up directly beneath him. The casting technique also allows an angler on crowded party boats to avoid tangles by tossing his lure away from the mass of vertically-dropped lines.

Regardless of how perfect and vertical your initial drop is, any lure will eventually—sometimes rapidly—drift away from the boat. After every few minutes of jigging, it's important to free-spool your lure to make contact with the bottom again. Otherwise, your jig will ride progressively higher in the water column and out of the strike zone as your line becomes increasingly more diagonal.

Due to the principles of geometry, the more diagonal your line becomes the greater amount of line you must release each time to reach bottom. You will soon reach a point when it's more efficient to reel your jig all the way in and start again with a new vertical drop. Also, most pros agree that jigs produce more strikes when fished as vertically as possible. Part of the reason may be the progressively less fluttering action as the drop angle increases.

Use a high-quality reel with a good free-spool to facilitate fast vertical drops and to help with casting. Most charter boat captains prohibit overhead casting for obvious safety reasons, so you'll need to learn to lob your jig underhanded. It's a good idea to practice this technique from a fishing pier or bridge before your trip. Learning to cast a 16-ounce jig sporting a treble hook and teaser when standing shoulder-to-shoulder with a bunch of strangers will be embarrassing at best.

A sporting, all-purpose bottomfish outfit (as opposed to a traditional extra-heavy action rod and rugged 4/0 reel), includes a 7-foot, medium-heavy rod rated for 20- to 40-pound line. Match your rod to a high-quality conventional 3/0 reel spooled with 40- to 50-pound super braid line. Levelwind models prove helpful for retrieving large amounts of line when fishing deep spots; however, speed of line retrieve is often of greater importance when selecting a reel. Some experts shun levelwinds because they believe that the mechanism slows a jig's sink rate.

There are many opinions about what makes an ideal codfishing rod. Many experienced cod anglers prefer medium-heavy, 7½- to 8-foot rods, for yo-yo style jigging because of their greater sweep and jig lifting ability. For squidding, which requires no rod lifting, a medium-heavy, 6½- to 7-foot length is all you need. Heavy- and extra-heavy-rated rods are not needed in most situations because the days of plentiful cow or "steaker" cod are over, and smaller market-size cod are now normal.

An excellent reel choice is one like a Shimano Calcutta TE700 levelwind loaded with 30- to 50-pound super braid line, although 30-pound line may prove too light when dogfish are present. A reel like a 4/0 Penn 113HN Senator is another good choice for water 250 to 400 feet deep because of its big spool and high gear ratio, and its economic price tag. Although top-end super braid lines are much more expensive than mono they are ideal for deepwater jigging due to their minimum diameter, high sensitivity and low stretch. They are a worthwhile investment.

Other codfish pros have different opinions regarding outfits. For example, some anglers feel you should select rods depending on whether you plan to use them on private and/or six-pack charter boats versus party boats, the principle difference being rod length. An ideal, all-purpose rod size for private and charter boats doesn't need to exceed 7 feet, however, a good length for a party boat rod is 7 to 8 feet long. Longer rods are preferable in tight quarters is because they provide greater casting distance and fewer tangles by keeping your line farther out from fellow anglers' rods. Factor in your intended fishing style when making a final selection.

Fishing on Stellwagen Bank in the Gulf of Maine, Derek DeSantis landed this pollock on soft-plastic teaser rigged above a diamond jig.

Rods with a softer tip offer better feel, whereas rods with a less-sensitive tip are better for working a heavy diamond jig in deep water. A jigging rod with a tip that's too soft won't impart much action to a large jig, especially when used with mono line, and will cause the angler to tire faster. A slow-action rod actually enhances jig action when using light to moderate-weight jigs fished with super braid line and in waters less than 200 feet deep. The reason is similar to how a fly rod works. When you initially and vigorously snap the rod upward it bends and "loads," the moment the rod tip reaches its apex, it releases its energy (the same way a bow fires an arrow) and briskly lifts the jig off the bottom. The angler then quickly lowers his rod to its starting point near the water, allowing the jig to free-fall with a horizontal fluttering action.

Wreck fishing, especially when the chance of big cod is a good possibility, requires a different rod performance. A shorter rod of 6 to 6½ feet provides the angler with better leverage and less "give" to impart pressure on a big fish and move it from the wreck before it bulldogs for freedom into the structure. This is a similar principle as when using short rods during stand-up battles with tuna or when trying to prevent grouper from diving into heavy structure.

Once again, braided line is the way to go for codfishing and is well worth the financial investment. The very act of yo-yo jigging with mono line in deep water means that with mono's 15 percent stretch, your vigorous rod lifts of 4 to 6 feet are absorbed by mono's elasticity and the lure's actual travel may be half that distance. Add in mono's lack of sensitivity, increased drag due to larger diameter and less abrasion resistance, and super braid is an all-round better choice.

9

BLACK SEA BASS

The black sea bass (*Centropristis striata*), not to be confused with other species of sea bass found around the word, is an excellent fish for eating. It is strictly a marine species and, unlike striped bass, doesn't migrate into estuaries to spawn. Because of its fine table qualities, commercial and recreational fishermen have largely overfished sea bass in recent years.

The black sea bass is technically a type of grouper (Serranidae family), which inhabits the coastal waters from Maine to Florida and the eastern Gulf of Mexico, and are especially popular with bottom fishermen from Rhode Island through Virginia. Many anglers catch sea bass in inshore waters like Long Island Sound, and though they range offshore to depths of over 400 feet in summer, they are most common in water less than 120 feet deep.

In winter sea bass migrate to depths of 600 and sometimes up to 1,000 feet. These fish inhabit areas close to bottom structure like artificial and natural reefs, mixed and rocky sea beds and wrecks, making any type of vertical relief a good place to target them.

On average, sea bass weigh about 1½ pounds, and the world record is about 9½ pounds, but any specimen over 5 pounds is noteworthy. Pros call large sea bass "humpbacks" or "humpies" because bigger specimens grow a significant hump behind their head, and although these sea bass are basically black, their color fluctuates according to the particular bottom they inhabit at the time.

Because sea bass prey includes baitfish and squid, large specimens will eagerly strike diamond-type jigs. Diamond, Butterfly-style, VI-KE, Crippled Herring and most other vertically-fished lures are good choices for deep-water situations where sea bass hold over wrecks or reefs.

Sea bass experts who fish deep water from private or party boats carry jigs ranging from 4 to 12 ounces; however, as with every other jigging situation use the lightest jig possible, which will allow the lure

Diamond jigs tipped with fresh bait are a viable option for big "hump-back" sea bass when fished over structure along the East Coast.

to have the most action and feel during the drop. Sea bass, like other species, often strike a jig as it falls. Don't be surprised if your falling jig stops short from a strike because sea bass sometimes suspend off the bottom.

A single 4/0 hook is about the right size for most sea bass, and you can make any vertical jig more appealing by attaching a white bucktail (not a bucktail jig, just a hook with hair dressing like a big saltwater fly) to it instead of a bare hook. Avoid using treble hooks because they injure small fish, hang bottom more often, are prone to foul hooking and create more tangles with fellow angler's lines. Some sea bass experts also tie a white bucktail dropper about 18 inches up from the jig. Both the dropper and jig hooks will catch better if tipped with a squid strip.

When fishing diamond-style jigs for sea bass, experiment with different types of retrieves such as squidding and yo-yo jigging, but these motions must be done slowly as described in the previous chapter on codfish. Always drop the lure quickly enough so that it turns horizontally and flutters on the drop, which will help induce strikes.

For offshore conditions use 30- to 40-pound braided line spooled on a 3/0 conventional reel matched to a medium-heavy conventional rod, and tie your jigs and dropper to 50-pound fluorocarbon. Although this gear may be overkill for sea bass, there's always a chance of hooking other big bottom dwellers like cod, bluefish, fluke, weakfish, grouper or striped bass, depending on the waters you fish.

10

YELLOWTAIL

As with the Eastern Seaboard, a wide variety of West Coast species respond well to diamond and other vertical jigs, however, rockfish (not to be confused with striped bass, which are sometimes called rockfish), yellowtail, ling cod, salmon and halibut comprise the main group of highly popular fish targeted by thousands of jig anglers from Alaska to the Mexican border.

Yellowtail

Yellowtail are a member of the Carangidae family and are closely related to jacks. They grow large, with an upper weight range reaching approximately 100 pounds, but the California record is about 80 pounds, and average fish are much smaller. Yellowtail are found from California southward to tropical waters and are a major target for Pacific deep-sea fishermen because of their fighting and eating qualities.

Yellowtail readily strike a range of baits and lures, but deep vertical jigging over reefs and pinnacles is a productive fishing method in their favored waters of up to 200 feet. During the past few decades, some yellowtail anglers have gravitated toward soft plastic lures; however, many fishermen still prefer dropping traditional iron jigs, often known as "candy-bar" type, and diamond jigs. More recently, the new Japanese flutter-style jigs have come into vogue and are also very attractive to yellowtail.

The basic yellowtail jigging technique involves using a modified yo-yo action, which begins by free-spooling a lure to the bottom. As soon as the jig stops free-falling, engage the reel and make three or four lifts and drops (yo-yo motion) of the rod tip, raising the tip sharply from a seven-o'clock to a ten o'clock position and giving the lure an upward jump of perhaps 4 or 5 feet. It's important to drop your rod tip quickly so the lure tumbles horizontally and flutters during the free fall. If you lower the rod too slowly some tension stays on the line and makes the jig drop vertically, which is actually a faster fall but one that doesn't stimulate as many strikes.

The snap-up and flutter-down motion is important because it simulates an injured baitfish or fleeing squid and triggers a strike on either the rise or drop of the lure. If no strike occurs after three or four sweeps, try a steady, fast retrieve to pull the lure up through the water column where suspended yellowtails frequently feed. Don't worry about reeling too quickly—it's unlikely you can crank faster than a yellowtail can swim.

When retrieving toward the surface, reel the jig only up through the fish-holding zone, which can vary significantly from day to day or spot to spot. For example, if you're fishing in 180 feet of water, the fish may be staging near the bottom, and the majority of yellowtails are being hooked in only the bottom-most 50 feet. Therefore, only reel your lure 50 to 60 feet off the bottom, rather than all the way to the top. This will save effort and time while keeping your jig in the strike zone. Because yo-yo jigging maintains the lure within a few feet of the bottom, you may also hook grouper, sea bass, rockfish or halibut.

Once you discover the depth at which yellowtail are holding, control the free-spool distance so your jig reaches the same depth on each drop. A simple way to do this is to count as the lure falls, such as of 1-2-3-4-5, etc., until you reach the number corresponding to the approximate depth you desire. If you first cast downwind or downtide, which is a common technique, remember the farther the cast the more slowly your lure will drop because it creates more line draped horizontally through the water. In other words, the belly in the line increases drag on the jig and slows its sink rate.

If you know exactly where the fish are holding by using a fishfinder, you can also measure off arm lengths (the distance from finger-tip to finger-tip is approximately your height) of line from your rod tip. Once you have pulled off 75 feet of line, for example, you can tie on waxed dental floss with a series of half-hitches so you can drop to that precise depth each time.

When a yellowtail grabs your jig, it's important to continue reeling and not set the hook until the fish has turned and is swimming away from you. Setting the hook too soon may pull the hook from the fish's mouth because it is facing upward as it chases the lure through the water column. According to most West Coast mates, you'll lose fewer fish by steady reeling after a strike, which eliminates slack and keeps the fish hooked.

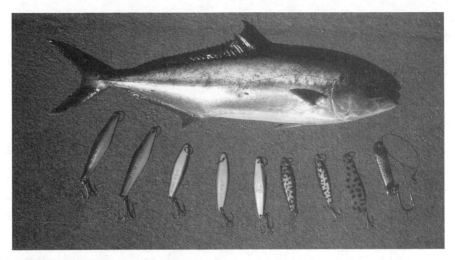

California yellowtail aggressively strike a wide variety of West Coast jigs cast to breaking fish or worked rapidly through the water column. *Photo by Doug Olander.*

Because vertical jigs require a fast retrieve to be effective, tackle usually includes a high-speed reel. A reel with a 4:1 gear ratio is usable, but a better choice is one with 5:1 or 5.5:1 gear ratio matched to a 6½-foot, fast-taper rod. The reel should hold at least 250 yards of 50-pound-test mono. The new wave of braided lines, however, has done a lot for jig fishermen, and spooling up with these super lines will allow you to use lighter jigs in deeper water during stronger currents. Some party and charter boats don't allow braids because of the complex tangles they can create.

When fishing is difficult and the yellowtails are finicky, anglers are increasingly turning to fluorocarbon leaders. Once in the water, fluorocarbon refracts less light, thereby making it less visible than monofilament. If you think the fish are around but simply aren't biting, try tying a 36- to 40-inch length of fluorocarbon onto the main line using double uni knots or a barrel swivel as a connector between the leader and main line.

Carry a variety of vertical jigs in your tackle box so you have a range of weights to choose from to match the conditions. Good options for lure patterns include a combination of blue/white, green/ yellow, chrome/blue, all-chrome and similar colorations.

11

ROCKFISH

Rockfish are another favorite West Coast sportfish that are extremely receptive to vertical jigging. These spiny critters are generally small, averaging 20 to 24 inches in length and not known for their fighting ability, however, they are excellent eating, and commercial interests have overfished the stocks in most areas. Many species of rockfish live along the West Coast, preferring craggy bottoms in depths of 200 to 700 feet.

Rockfish react well to vertical lures, and two of the most popular styles are heavy models of traditional diamond jigs and standard West Coast hex bar jigs. Due to the great depths that rockfish inhabit, lures of high density and weight are needed to reach them.

Be aware there are depth regulations you must adhere to. In some northern zones, you may not catch or possess rockfish (or lingcod) in waters greater than 180 feet deep. Fishing to this depth still requires the use of fairly heavy jigs but not nearly as heavy as when anglers fished in waters of 400 feet or more. The central zones allow fishing in waters of 240 feet or less, and southern zones permit fishing in depths of 360 feet or less. These regulations impact the weight of jigs you need to carry but are always subject to change, so check the latest regulations before heading out.

For the shallower zones, the most popular vertical lures are 2- to 6-ounce diamond jigs and hex bars. Tackle shops often sell these without hooks, and local fishermen use a split ring to attach size 1/0-3/0 trebles. However, treble hooks greatly increase bottom snags when jigging over structure. To avoid that problem, rig your jigs with a single 2/0 Siwash hook. As rockfish shake and twist on the way to the surface they fight against the weight of a heavy jig and can tear it from their mouth. To help correct this drawback, attach a barrel swivel between the jig and the hook so the fish can spin or shake without leveraging against the dead weight of the lure.

Rockfish love jigs worked against deep structure along the Pacific coast.
Photo by Doug Olander.

The standard rockfish jigging technique starts with casting or lob-bing a jig in the direction of your boat's drift and then immediately re-leasing line as the lure sinks. The purpose of the cast is to "lead" the boat in the direction it's travelling. In other words, by casting down-tide and/or downwind, your jig will reach the bottom nearer the same time the boat reaches that spot from above. If you lower your jig straight down from the gunnel, as some novices do, the current will sweep your jig under the boat and offer a poor, diagonal jigging angle right from the start of your drop.

As soon as your jig hits bottom, engage the reel and snap it up by briskly lifting your rod tip. Drop your rod tip again so the jig flutters to the bottom and repeat, reeling in slack line in the process. Strikes often occur on the drop, which are usually indicated by sudden slack line as if you had just lost your lure. Some species of rockfish travel off the structure and up the water column; therefore, yo-yo jigging combined with a retrieve is sometimes productive.

12

LINGCOD

Lingcod, or ling, are widely distributed in ocean waters along the West Coast from Alaska to southern California. Their ideal habitat consists of rocks and/or kelp in depths of less than 400 feet. Because ling lack an airbladder, anglers can safely release those caught in depths of over 300 feet.

The name lingcod is misleading because this fish isn't related to true cod; however, they are the largest member of the greenling family. Ling can live to approximately 25 years old, grow to over 50 pounds and reach over 4 feet in length.

Ling are voracious feeders, sometimes grabbing other hooked lingcod almost their size and holding onto them long enough for a boat's mate to gaff or net them at the surface. They will attack and eat almost any creature they can catch, but they favor herring, squid and various small bottomfish. Ling are very aggressive and, if enticed, will charge away from their rocky habitat and chase forage or a lure to the surface. This relentless aggression combined with excellent eating quality makes these predators very popular with vertical-jig fishermen.

Effective vertical jigs for lingcod are available in a wide variety of shapes, colors and sizes. They are all designed to plummet to the bottom, and most feature treble hooks. These lures range from standard West Coast solid-metal bars to traditional East Coast diamond jigs. Some ling fishermen customize these otherwise plain jigs with special paints, reflective tapes and over-size single hooks. Ling have large mouths, so they have no trouble inhaling a big hook. Single hooks are advantageous because they reduce bottom snags and allow easier releases for the angler with less damage to the fish.

The new breed of colorful, flutter-style jigs are rapidly becoming popular with West Coast anglers. These jigs are extremely effective for ling fishing because of their deep-drop capabilities combined with

Lingcod, no relation to Atlantic cod, are aggressive predators that will at times chase a metal jig or another hooked fish up through the water column. *Photo by Doug Olander.*

enhanced horizontal action. Typical weights for traditional ling jigs range from 8 to 16 ounces, and they are best fished with a steady yo-yo motion, using large sweeps of the rod. Occasionally reeling up 10 turns may cause ling to dash after a jig, believing it's escaping prey.

The wide variety of productive lingcod jigs is matched with the equally wide variety of lingcod rods. For "shallow" water of less than 200 feet, a medium-weight 6½- to 7-foot rod and conventional 3/0-size reel loaded with 25- to 30-pound braid works well. At depths greater than 200 feet with correspondingly larger jigs, a medium-heavy rod and 4/0-size reel spooled with 40- to 65-pound braid is preferable. Some anglers like to top-shot their braid with a length of mono for less visibility and better shock absorption. It's a good idea to run a couple of feet of 80-pound mono abrasion leader between the main line and the jig to help avoid bite-offs from lings' sharp teeth.

There are many dependable and suitable reels for ling fishing. Popular choices for depths of 100-400 feet include reels with deep spools and a sturdy levelwind in sizes 3/0 and 4/0. Examples of these outfits include Penn's Graphite Super Levelwind, Senator and International and Shimano's Charter Special, TLD, Tekota and non-levelwind Trinidad.

13

HALIBUT

Pacific halibut weigh from 20 to over 300 pounds, but any fish over 100 pounds is considered a trophy. Those weighing over 90 pounds are almost always female, however, because they grow much larger than do males. Halibut are aggressive, striking flatfish that feed on a variety of small bottomfish, squid and octopus. One of their favorite foods is herring, and that's a reason why vertical jigs—which resemble herring—are so effective for catching halibut.

Halibut prefer habitats abundant with forage where they are able to lie and ambush unsuspecting prey. Bottom depressions or basins are good places to look for these big flatties, as are slopes rising from deep water. Underwater humps, plateaus and sharp drop-offs are ideal places to jig because this is where baitfish hold or are pushed into striking range by the current. Anglers commonly work these slopes by drifting with the tide so they move along the slope from higher ground to deeper water.

As with many other types of deepwater angling, jigging is the simplest and most effective technique to catch halibut. Heavy slab, hex bar, pipe and deep-drop jigs are popular. Other favorite halibut jigs include Luhr Jensen's Crippled Herring and the traditional Bridgeport-style diamond. All are productive when used in sizes heavy enough to reach bottom in water 100 to 600 feet deep. In those depths, jigs of 12 to 32 ounces may be necessary.

Because halibut rest against the ocean floor—usually on areas composed of gravel or cobble—waiting for forage to be swept past, hitting the bottom continually with your jig is an important key to consistently catching these massive flatfish. The typical fishing technique is to yo-yo the jig with long, upward sweeps and quick drops of your rod tip, being sure the lure hits bottom on each drop. This rod movement gives the jig a tight wobbling action as it rockets upward several feet, followed by an erratic fluttering action during its free-

Pacific Northwest halibut like large, lead-headed bucktail jigs tipped with bait or soft plastic and bounced along the bottom. *Photo by Jackie Olander.*

fall, simulating spawning or injured baitfish and prompting instinctive strikes. Halibut often hit jigs as they fall, so be prepared to set the hook during the drop.

Typical deep-water halibut tackle includes a 7-foot, heavy-action boat rod and conventional 4/0 reel spooled with 300 yards of 50- to 80-pound super braid line. Braids excel in these conditions for their sensitivity, thin diameter, low stretch and high strength.

14

SALMON

Pacific salmon is a term used to describe members of the salmonidae family found in the Pacific Northwest region of the country. There are five members of this group living in these northern waters; chinook, coho, pink, sockeye and chum. Salmon are one of the most sought-after fish species in the world, both recreationally and commercially. However, the most desired and frequently caught types are coho and chinook.

Salmon are an ancient fish as evidenced by fossil remains over 100 million years old. They prefer cold, fast, oxygen-rich waters and spend a large part of their life in the ocean before migrating upriver to spawn. Most fish taken recreationally are caught when staging in preparation to spawn, such as near river mouths, because that's when they're most concentrated and accessible.

Pacific salmon typically feed at mid-depths on small, silvery fish like herring, candlefish and sand lance, which means they're natural candidates for vertical jigging. This type of fishing occurs in saltwater, however, and not in rivers. The depths at which salmon congregate varies considerably. Coho, for instance, are found from surface level down to as much as 50 to 100 feet. Chinook also gather at the surface, but are more often found in depths of 60 to 150 or more feet deep.

Vertical jigging, by nature, doesn't cover a wide area of water like trolling or casting does. Therefore, jigging is most effective when you find a concentration of salmon working baitfish. Once you've located a school with your depthfinder, you must stay over them, turning off your motor so as not to spook them but moving back into position when pushed off by the tide or wind.

As you drop your lure through the fish, it's important to maintain your line in as vertical an attitude as possible. As your line becomes increasingly diagonal due to the tide or wind action, you should reel back up to the surface and start a new vertical drop. The reason this is important is that salmon often strike as a lure falls. When dropped quickly and vertically, a jig turns sideways and flutters or falls erratically in a more horizontal fashion. As your line becomes more diagonal, it necessarily requires you to let out more line to maintain the same depth. This additional line length and angle creates drag in the current and prevents the jig from fluttering.

Salmon respond well to traditional diamond jigs and vertical-jig/spoon hybrids like Luhr Jensen's Crippled Herring, but any of the wide variety of new Japanese flutter-style jigs are also extremely effective. These various jigs work on the same general principle. They catch salmon because they are thin, fluttering, falling slabs of shiny metal that make predators react instinctively and strike. Some of these jigs are designed so anglers can bend them for varying action. While this may be beneficial for a cast or trolled lure, the bend may reduce or negate much of the horizontal fluttering action that's so attractive.

As with all other types of vertical jigging, select the lightest lure possible for the conditions. Jig size will vary by depth. For coho, you'll generally need 1 to 3 ounces. Chinook usually require heavier

Try working conventional or flutter-style jigs under schools of salmon for red hot action on light tackle. This salmon fell for the jig seen hanging across its lower jaw. *Photo by Doug Olander.*

jigs of 2 to 6 ounces or more, always starting with a jig of only a few ounces and working up from there, but those in the 2- to 3-ounce range are most useful and considered to be the all-purpose size. If your lure quickly drifts off in a diagonal direction during the drop, it's time to switch to a heavier jig to allow for a more vertical fall.

Most vertical jigging for salmon is done with a short yo-yo motion and not with speed squidding where the jig is cranked up very quickly for 10 or more turns. Once your jig is in the strike zone, usually determined by a good fishfinder or the captain's suggestion, work your rod tip up in slow sweeps of 18 to 24 inches and then drop the tip fast enough for the lure to flutter as it falls. Don't create too much slack on the drop because you should stay in fairly close contact with your rig at all times.

A majority of hits occur as the lure falls like a wounded baitfish or spawning herring, including during long free-spools to the depth you seek. When a salmon grabs the lure, the sensation is as if the jig hit bottom prematurely because the line suddenly goes slack. Work your rod close to the water, rather than at shoulder height, so you have room to lift the rod for a quick hook-set.

A 7- to 8-foot rod with medium action and a sensitive tip makes a good choice for jigging light- to medium-weight jigs. A rod that's too light, however, will fish with a constant bend when using a heavy jig. This will prevent a hard hook set when a salmon strikes because the rod is already loaded.

As with other types of vertical jigging, a high speed conventional reel is less tiresome for the angler. A size 2/0 reel with a retrieve ratio of 4:1 to 5.5:1 and a good drag system is essential. Lighter reels, however, including those freshwater types used for bass and walleye, will also work and are a lot of fun when spooled with only 12-pound line. Because salmon are suspended off the bottom, a reel with a levelwind and line counter is very useful to help you keep your jig within the strike zone. The consensus on spinning outfits is mixed. Some anglers say they can set the hook better, while other fishermen say that spinning outfits should be reserved for casting, not for vertical jigging. The decision is left to personal choice.

Mono line will work adequately for shallow water, but for deep vertical jigging in depths of 100 feet or more, super braid line is well worth the investment. It offers a thinner diameter, increased sensitivity, better strength and low stretch. Ultimately, the reduced line drag will allow you to fish lighter jigs for better action.

Some anglers use 30-pound mono backing on the reel and then top-shot it with 100 to 200 yards of super braid line rated at 30- to 50-

pound test. You can tie on a 4-foot section mono or fluorocarbon leader using a double uni-knot or a high-quality barrel swivel. Mono, with its 15 percent stretch, helps absorb some of the impact of a hard strike and thereby reduces hook pullouts. The stiff leader material also helps reduce the limp braid line from tangling in the hook as the jig flutters down.

Many vertical jigs, such as the Point Wilson Dart Jig, come factory-rigged with a treble hook. If you are planning to fish the mid-depth range and will be keeping your catch, treble hooks are your best bet for landing feisty salmon, but if you are fishing areas where jigs are bounced off the bottom and worked up through the water column, you'll have fewer snags by changing out trebles to singles.

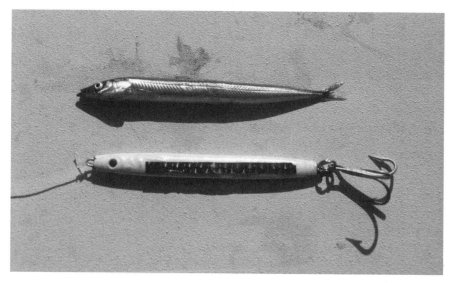

Lures such as the popular and productive Point Wilson Dart Jig perfectly imitate local salmon forage like candlefish and sand eels. You can tune-up any jig by adding holographic tape for more reflection. *Photo by Doug Olander.*

Likewise, some areas of the West Coast may require the use of single or barbless hooks, so be sure to check local game and fish regulations before heading out. A good single-hook option is a 4/0 Siwash. One trick some jigging pros use is to attach two Siwash hooks, face to face, on the same split ring or barrel swivel at the bottom of the lure. This configuration will increase the hook-up potential and reduce the snagging tendencies of fixed treble hooks. Using single hooks, rather than treble hooks, also reduces the chances of snagging the leader during the fall.

Even if you purchase the jig with a single Siwash, it's often wise to replace it with a slightly larger size for better hooking ability. As when vertical-jig fishing for other species, rigging a barrel swivel between the hook and the jig, usually by means of a heavy-duty split ring, will help prevent salmon from using the leverage of the jig to tear the hook out.

15

BOTTOMFISH AND PELAGICS

Few tackle shops around the Gulf of Mexico, especially along Florida's West Coast, sell diamond jigs. Compared to the Northeast and West Coasts, not many anglers fish vertical jigs on the bottom, preferring instead to work heavy bucktails for species like grouper and snapper.

Diamond jigs, however, can be effective for predators like amberjacks and grouper when fished over artificial reefs or small, natural outcroppings with a yo-yo jigging motion and tackle similar to that used when fishing bucktails. Some experts add a soft plastic curly tail to a single hook rigged to a diamond jig. The added flutter prompts many predators into striking. Both yo-yo jigging and squidding are productive for jacks, whereas grouper and large snapper need a jig to stay close to the bottom with a slow-speed yo-yo motion of only 2 to 4 feet.

Diamond jigs are popular with offshore anglers working around any of the numerous platforms and oil rigs scattered in the Gulf of Mexico, and many of them have become important fish attractors. The reason is because they provide artificial structure, similar to artificial reefs, on an otherwise nondescript Gulf bottom that's composed primarily of sand and mud.

The stanchions and legs of offshore rigs start a food chain by accumulating marine growth such as tiny crustaceans, mollusks and sea weeds. Baitfish feed on the forage and they, in turn, draw predators such as tuna. Jigging against the bottom near offshore rigs is often impossible because many are over 100 miles offshore and in waters ranging from 2,000 to over 12,000 feet deep.

Finding productive oil rigs or platforms is challenging. Fishing reports, of course, are important. Experienced anglers also use one or more of the sea surface temperature charts mentioned in the appendix to pick the most likely rigs to fish. Clear water and good currents are other important factors for determining which rigs are best to explore.

Gag grouper respond well to a variety of metal jigs fished deep against structure in southern waters. *Photo by Doug Olander.*

Both diamond- and butterfly-type jigs work well around platforms, and you should start with the lightest jig possible, usually one between 4 and 6 ounces, rigged to 3 to 5 feet of 50-pound fluorocarbon leader. Spool a high-quality conventional reel with 30- to 50-pound mono attached to a 6½-foot, stand-up rod rated from 20- to 50-pound class, depending on the size of fish you expect.

Free spool the jig to the thermocline or to whatever depth you are marking fish on your electronics. As with tuna fishing in the Northeast use a fast yo-yo jigging motion by snapping your rod tip up above your head and then dropping the tip fast enough to create slack so the jig flutters as it falls. Tuna hits often occur as the lure tumbles like a wounded baitfish, so be ready for a strike on the drop. If this technique fails to produce a hit, use a lift-drop-retrieve combination to work your lure up through the water column to the surface.

Dangling or dancing stinger hooks rigged butterfly style and traditional treble hooks are both good choices for a jig. In years past, however, some treble hooks would break off at the eye when heavily loaded and pushed to the limit by tuna and other tough fish. Some anglers believed that the hooks were actually designed to sacrifice themselves this way when hung on the bottom so you would lose the hook but recover the jig, but according to Capt. Greg Metcalf, previous owner of Bridgeport Diamond Jigs, this was never true. Any hook can fail when pressured to its limit.

In its Bridgeport Diamond Jig collection, Uncle Josh sells a heavy-duty "Jig-for-Rigs" version of its standard diamond jig. The lure is designed specifically for tuna, amberjack and other strong pelagics. Peter Renkert, Dana Pickup's former partner (owners of Bridgeport Diamond Jigs and Bead Tackle before Greg Metcalf), and a dealer from Louisiana developed the Jig for Rigs for specialty anglers fishing around oil rigs in the Gulf of Mexico.

The design team used a solid-eye Mustad treble hook and attached it to the jig with a heavy-duty Rosco split ring to prevent break-offs during high pressure situations. The jigs are available in five weights from 3 to 10 ounces and four colors: nickel, white, yellow and red. The one possible drawback to this lure, however, is the lack of a swivel between the jig and treble hook. Although the Jig-for-Rigs lure has excellent holding power, some vertical-jig anglers prefer a swivel connection to help counteract fish twisting and leveraging against the jig's weight. But, that is personal preference.

School tuna are prime targets when using vertical jigs offshore around platforms or down in the thermocline.

16

PARTY BOATS—BLUEFISH, COD AND TUNA

Party boats, also called head boats, have nothing to do with a festive celebration at sea, and are called party boats because their customers often board in groups or parties. The term head boat refers to the way owners or captains charge or count individuals boarding their boat, which is per person or by the head. Charters, conversely, charge one rate for the entire boat.

Party boats are large vessels, averaging from 60 to 120 feet in length, fishing either nearshore or offshore for species ranging from 2-pound porgies to 200-pound tuna. Many such boats operate from all our coasts and may stay at sea anywhere from a half day to two

Party boats are perfect for anglers not owning their own boat but who would like to catch fish with vertical jigs. Note the mate landing the big bluefish with a long-handled gaff near the stern.

weeks, depending on their distance offshore and targeted species. The benefit of fishing from a party boat is they almost always catch fish and, because they accommodate anywhere from 50 to 100 or more patrons, their individual trip rates are inexpensive compared to private charter boats, which are licensed to carry a maximum of only six anglers. If you have a large enough party, many head-boat owners allow you to privately hire the entire vessel for a day of fishing.

Party boats also differ from charter boats because once aboard a party boat you're mostly on your own. On a charter boat, because of the small ratio of mates to anglers, there is a lot more attention and one-on-one instruction given throughout the entire fishing process.

For predators like bluefish, cod and tuna, two common techniques used aboard party boats are bait fishing and diamond jigging. While bait fishing is productive and fairly simple, it has its drawbacks. Customers must bait their own hooks—a time consuming and messy process, bottom snags and tangles are common and fish are often gut hooked. Generally, beginners use bait while seasoned party-boat anglers frequently switch to diamond jigs because of their high catch rate, faster turnaround time and cleaner operation.

If you're new to the party boat game, it's important to know how the systems work. Otherwise you, the mates, and the surrounding fishermen will quickly become frustrated with your ineptitude. Although it's impossible to cover all types of party boats and their specific species here, I'll review some general practices, techniques and recommendations to get you started for a productive future of offshore vertical jigging.

Many half-day head boats are "walk on," meaning they don't require reservations, while trips of longer duration usually do require reservations and credit card deposits, so call ahead to check that first. Plan to arrive approximately an hour before sailing time to purchase your ticket and save a spot, especially if travelling with a group of buddies.

Tackle isn't always included in the trip fee. If it's not, you'll have the choice of renting tackle—usually $5 to $10 for the trip—from the boat crew or you may bring your own gear. If you choose to bring your rod and reel, check in advance to determine that it's suitable for the expected conditions and species. A good, all-purpose outfit is a medium-heavy 7-foot boat rod and heavy-duty, no frills conventional reel such as a 3/0 or 4/0 Penn Senator filled with 50-pound-test line. Most head boat customers use mono, but this is an ideal application for the new super braids because they offer zero stretch, high sensitivity and less water resistance. Braids outperform mono in every jigging situation except tuna fishing.

Many head boats sell burlap sacks to hold your fish, but leave your fillet knife in the car. Mates make their money from tips and filleting fees; therefore, patrons are not permitted to fillet their fish while on-board—but you're free to carry your catch off the boat whole if you prefer.

Next, after buying your ticket and boarding the vessel, ask a mate what areas around the boat are permissible to fish from. Don't be surprised if the "regulars" have arrived extra early and already claimed the best spots, which are usually around the bow and the stern. If that's the case, settle in somewhere amidships and mark your spot with your rod by tying it in place against the rail with a wipe rag. Then you can sit down and enjoy the ride out to sea.

Like any other saltwater fishing boat, a party boat may troll, drift or anchor to fish. In a drifting scenario, such as when bluefishing in fast water like the famous Race at the mouth of Long Island Sound, have your rod ready with a diamond jig of appropriate weight. Usually a jig of 8 to 12 ounces rigged with a single 8/0 hook is a good starting choice for most deepwater situations. And, of course, you can always call ahead for specific tackle advice. Avoid jigs rigged with treble hooks because they snag bottom and other anglers' lines much more easily.

You can tie a jig directly to your main line if you're fishing heavy mono or you can run about four feet of 80-pound-mono abrasion leader in front of the lure and attach that to the main line via a heavy-duty barrel swivel. Some party boats, and many charter boats, prohibit super braid because it's so difficult to untangle. If you want to fish braid, call ahead for approval.

Once the boat arrives at the fishing grounds wait until the captain signals before dropping your jig into the depths, otherwise you risk tangling your line in the propeller. Free spool your lure to the bottom, immediately engage the reel and begin a jigging process. Frequently, underhanded casting downwind or downtide is a good technique to help overcome the boat's drift.

For species like bluefish and striped bass, the jigging technique is usually squidding, which means hitting bottom, taking 10 fast turns up, releasing the line, hitting bottom again and continuing the drop/retrieve cycle. You can also use the squidding technique for codfish and haddock, but they are more sluggish and you must crank the 10 turns much more slowly. Codfishing with diamond jigs is also accomplished with a yo-yo jigging motion, which simply means hitting bottom, engaging the reel, taking a few turns up to clear any hangs and then working the jig up and down only by lifting and lowering your rod tip with long sweeps.

Raquel Kellert proudly displays her personal-best bluefish, a 16-pounder, landed on a party boat fishing in the Race at the eastern entrance of Long Island Sound. Large diamond jigs and heavy tackle are required in such areas due to the deep water and strong currents.

While you're fishing, the boat may be drifting over rough ground. These passes will often take your lure up a shoaling reef, across its crest and down its backside. For good catch rates, you must keep your lure near the bottom—the closer the better—while moving over the varying terrain and depths. When yo-yo jigging be sure you periodically free-spool your lure to the bottom to stay in the strike zone.

If your jig hangs on the structure below—and sooner or later it will—there's no motoring back uptide to free it as might happen in a private boat. Quickly lock down the spool and point the rod in the direction of the line. Hold on tightly and wait for the jig to come free or the line to part. Never grab the line and take a turn around your hand—even with a rag—because that's inviting severed fingers. It's a good idea to keep a wooden dowel in your tackle bag; take a few wraps of the braid around the dowel when trying to free a snagged line. After the lure is broken off, tie on a new jig and accept it as part of the head-boat routine.

When a big fish grabs the hook you're in for a hard fight and possibly some tangles as the tough critter darts around your fellow anglers' lines. Don't lighten the drag to have more fun and play the fish. This isn't a light-tackle sporting event—just winch it to the surface as fast as possible. The more leeway you give the fish the more mess it will create around other lines.

Once your catch has surfaced don't attempt to lift it from the water. Call for a mate who'll hurry over with a long-handled gaff or net and boat the fish for you. The mate may also unhook your fish, if needed, and untangle any crossed lines. Then you're on your own again.

At the end of each pass or drift the captain sounds the horn, and everyone immediately reels in his or her line. Don't delay! The boat can't steam back uptide or upwind until all hooks are aboard. To be fair to everyone else, the captain will usually alternate the side of the boat that faces downtide on each drift. This process means that half the time your line will be running under the boat, and half the time your line will be running away from the boat.

If your party boat anchors over a piece of prime structure, such as a wreck or artificial reef, your jigging options are the same except that the boat won't be moved repeatedly to drift over the hot spot. You have a good chance of catching a big cod or grouper feeding near the structure or, say, a pollock or jack hovering above it.

Trolling from a head boat usually occurs when hunting for fast-swimming pelagic species like tuna or king mackerel. If you choose to try diamond jigging when the boat is trolling, your fishing won't begin until one or more fish are hooked off the stern and the boat stops its forward momentum.

Capt. Jeff Gutman, operator of the party boat *Voyager* sailing from Point Pleasant Beach, New Jersey, suggested many excellent tips and helpful procedures when trolling or chunking and then jigging for tuna.

He believes trolling is an effective method of catching tuna, but whether the boat trolls or not depends on the conditions and isn't done on every trip. For obvious logistical reasons, not everybody aboard a head boat can troll a rod at once, so when you're in the group not trolling you should plan to jig for tuna. When one or more bites occur on the trolled lines, the boat will continue moving for a half minute to try to get hits on the other lures. Then the captain will pull the boat out of gear and slow it to a stop—this is when you should be ready at the rail with a diamond jigging outfit.

For an appropriate jigging combination, it is almost impossible to work a lure all day with a short, heavy stand-up rod and big 6/0 reel like those used for chunking or trolling. A good all-purpose jigging outfit for school tuna is a 3/0 or 4/0 conventional reel with high-quality drag and a matching, medium-heavy to heavy 6½-foot rod. Spool your reel with 50- to 60-pound-test line. For tuna, it's best to fish with monofilament rather than braid because of its stretch and shock-absorbing qualities.

Attach a high-quality 4- to 12-ounce vertical-drop lure, such as a diamond, Hopkins, Crippled Herring or VI-KE jig rigged with a single, heavy-duty 7/0 to 9/0 Siwash hook attached to the jig via a heavy-duty split ring and a sturdy barrel swivel. Flutter-style lures, such as Shimano's Butterfly Jigs, or those marketed by SPRO, Williamson and Braid, are also very effective, and fishermen have success with the dancing assist hooks rigged at the front of these lures. In fact, some tuna experts rig *all* their jigs—even traditional diamond jigs—with assist hooks from the head and remove those hooks (single or treble) trailing from the tail end. Small bucktail jigs can be productive and are sometimes used when casting to dolphin from party boats.

As the boat slows to a stop and the hooked-up anglers are busy fighting their fish, drop or cast your jig off the upwind side of the boat and start jigging. For safety reasons, don't cast overhand unless you are specifically told you may do so. Listen for the captain to announce the ideal depth to jig because he can often see the tuna on his color depthfinder.

Like jigging for other species, there are two basic fishing methods you can use for tuna. One difference, however, is that you'll be fish-

Party boat fishing can become congested and hectic at times. But it's always fun, and action is almost guaranteed. Toss your jig out away from the crowd to help avoid tangles and get the best vertical drops.

ing at a mid-water depth rather than off the bottom. You may either free-spool your lure to the proper depth and yo-yo jig by raising and lowering your rod tip in long, sharp sweeps, or you may free-spool your lure to the right depth and squid or retrieve your jig as fast as possible for about 10 turns. Tuna often strike during the lure drop, so be prepared for a vicious hit as the lure flutters down.

You can also jig for tuna from an anchored party boat while others are bait chunking, and most captains will encourage you to try it. According to Capt. Gutman, jigging is often the most productive way to catch school tuna aboard party boats, and he frequently sees jig fishermen out-fish everyone else onboard.

If the vessel is resting at anchor and you want to jig, don't try to do it while you already have a baitfishing line overboard. You must choose one technique or the other but not both. Otherwise, a mate will tell you to reel in your bait rod and stow it.

Once you have a strike, you must walk around the rail to follow your tuna or other big pelagic. Try to keep a 90-degree angle to the boat's rail with your rod and line; in other words, don't let the fish pull your line diagonally to your left or right because it will increase tangles with other lines. Likewise, if another fisherman is hooked into a tuna and must walk toward you, get out of his way as quickly as possible. The person fighting the fish will need to go over you and your rod. Help him by pointing your rod down at the water and ducking or moving wherever the mate tells you.

Never leave your rod unattended at the rail, which goes for any type of party boat fishing, not just for tuna. If you have to use the head or want to walk into the cabin for a snack or drink, always reel in your line and move your rod out of the way. Otherwise, a mate will simply cut the line of any unattended rod and remove it.

If you're fishing for smaller fish like bluefish or cod, you can slip your catch into a burlap sack or cooler, but when you've landed a tuna, quickly cut your line at the hook and hand the mate one of your pre-labeled fish tags, which will identify your fish at trip's end. The mate will then take your fish to the stern, clean it, attach a tag and place the body in the ice hold. A mate may ask you to carry your own fish to the stern during a hot bite, so cooperate whenever needed.

Once you're back at the dock, be sure to generously tip the mates before you leave the vessel. The mates work long and hard to enable your success, and they earn most of their income from tips and filleting fees.

17

NEW BREED LURES—FLUTTER, DEEP-DROP AND BALL JIGS

Far different from regular diamond jigs, a new wave of lures, collectively known as flutter, butterfly and deep-drop jigs—terms often, but incorrectly, used interchangeably—have some similarities to other vertically-fished jigs, however, these cutting-edge products are designed to fish differently from standard heavy-metal lures. Flutter and deep-drop jigs brought the most significant change in vertical jigging since John Schmuke first produced diamond jigs in Bridgeport, Connecticut, in the mid 1920s. These new jigs work well on a wide variety of bottom and mid-water fish and are used successfully off all our coasts.

Butterfly jigs are technically a brand name series of lures made by Shimano, and the term shouldn't be used to describe flutter and deep-drop jigs from other companies and their similar function and appearance. Deep-drop jigs differ from flutter jigs in their shape and balance, which affect the way they perform. A tail-heavy design shapes deep-drop jigs thick toward the base and tapered near the head. These elongated-tear-drop-shaped lures plummet tail-first and vertically into the depths with great speed and little resistance, making them ideal for working over deep bottom structure and in swift currents. Deep-drop jigs achieve their action on the retrieve, especially when combined with specific rod-and-reel methods.

Deep-drop jigs were created in Japan in the early 1990s to catch bluefin tuna in waters up to 500 feet deep. The Japanese were able to fish these great depths by using these jigs in combination with the first generation of super braid lines and fluorocarbon shock leaders. From Japan, the technique spread rapidly around the world, and now anglers in North America, South America, Africa and Australia use a variety of these deep-water lures.

Similar to deep-drop lures, flutter jigs are flatter, longer and more neutrally weighted than their sister deep-drop jigs. Their shape and central weight distribution allow them to "float" into the depths, dropping horizontally and fluttering downward like a wounded fish. With the proper rod-and-reel techniques their action occurs on both the drop and retrieve. Flutter jigs perform best in moderate depths with light currents. The forerunner of the modern-day flutter-style jig was probably Norway's Solvkroken Stingsilder herring jig, which became available in the United States in the 1960s. The Stingsilder is somewhat flat, neutrally balanced and has a detailed, enamel finish and fish-like shape.

Flutter and deep-drop jigs are available in many shapes, holographic colors, lengths and weights. Weights can range from 2 to 14 ounces, while lengths can range from 3½ to 9½ inches. The main distinguishing features of these jigs are their special shape, center-of-gravity and hook configuration.

A third possible design, which some companies also produce, is a weight-forward metal jig. Front-weighted jigs have wider and/or thicker heads and tapered tails. When properly fished, these lures

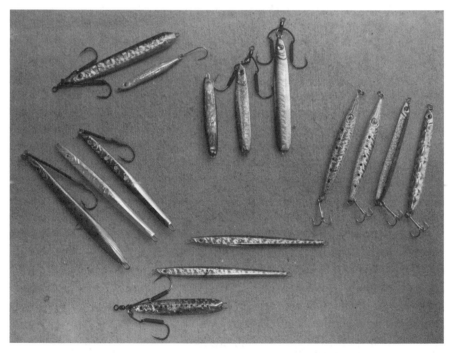

A growing number of tackle manufacturers are making flutter- and deep-drop-style jigs. Clockwise from the far left are jig examples made by Williamson, Tormenter, Spro, Colman's and Shimano. *Photo by Maggie Migdalski.*

rise and fall head-first for a special undulating action. The secret to achieving the head-first fall is to drop your rod tip fast enough to eliminate vertical line drag, thereby allowing the head to fall toward the bottom. These lures are usually rigged with single or treble tail hooks.

The unusual hook arrangement of flutter-style jigs consists of one or two (two is the maximum permissible by IGFA regulations) dangling hooks known variously as dangling, stinger or assist hooks—typically short-shank, wide-gap, single types—tethered to a solid O-ring by a short length of Dacron, Spectra, Kevlar or wire.

New to the market are dangling treble hooks. The Mustad hook company, for example, now makes a black-nickel 3x strong treble hook in sizes 1/0 and 3/0. It's attached to a 90-pound-test, 1.9-inch, 49-strand wire leader, which features a barrel swivel crimped onto the lure end.

The leader ties onto the same O-ring above the lure as does the dangling hook. A heavy-duty split ring secures the O-ring to the jig head. Thus, the hooks dangle from a fixed point above the jig rather than from its base. However, some anglers prefer to attach a standard J hook to the jig's tail end when fishing for certain species like bluefish, but there are several good reasons for head-rigged assist hooks.

First, various predators swallow their prey whole or attack it from the front, rather than the tail. For example, striped bass swallow baitfish whole and head-first, versus bluefish, which bite their prey in half from the tail. Thus, a rear-attached J hook would be a better choice for bluefishing, which would also help keep a bluefish's sharp teeth farther from the leader.

Second, many deep-swimming predators, like striped bass, cod and grouper, which lack large teeth, inhale their prey rather than severing it. Dangling assist hooks are especially effective for them because the hooks are, obviously, lighter than the jig. When a fish opens its mouth to strike the lure, it inhales the hooks first.

Third, when a J or treble hook is attached directly to the tail of a jig, a hooked fish can twist against the weight of the lure, thereby leveraging the hook from its mouth.

Last, if a fish strikes and feels the sting of a J or treble without becoming hooked, it won't return for another shot, but with dangling assist hooks, if a predator hits the tail of the jig but misses the hook, it will often return and strike again.

Choose assist hooks with gaps wider than the jig's body to prevent them from snagging on the fluttering lure. Also, you should pick the assist hook's tether length according to jig size. The hook shouldn't dangle farther down than the jig's midpoint. Long hook shanks and tethers reduce an assist hook's mobility. Short tethers, on the other hand, enable hooks to swing more freely and allow the jig to perform better.

Experienced charter captains usually prefer a single, rather than double assist-hook configuration. The reason is because fish often get only one hook caught in their mouth, then the second hook, still swinging free, lodges in the cheek during the fight and creates a bridle effect. The result is a diagonal pull, which simulates a foul-hooked fish.

Smaller flutter jigs are also excellent to cast to breaking fish like school tuna, false albacore, jacks and bluefish. In this application, however, remove the stinger hook and attach a treble hook to the jig's tail end via a heavy duty split ring and barrel swivel. Try a rapid retrieve first, and if that fails to produce hits use a stop-and-go action with rod tip pulls to simulate an injured baitfish, but for vertical jigging, some pros feel that a tail-attached hook affects the jig's fluttering action and you should avoid it.

The big question is this: Will these various new breed lures really perform better than standard bucktails and diamond jigs? That depends on which expert you ask and what species and fishing style you are after. These new jigs are certainly another available tool in your tackle box. The more options and experience you have the better you can tailor techniques and tackle to a specific fishing application on a given day. If the bluefish are marauding in a shallow rip and would eagerly bite a spark plug, there's little sense in using—and probably losing—an expensive, fluttering jig when a cheaper diamond jig will work wonders. On the other hand, in deep water or when targeting less numerous and fussier fish, a flutter-style jig may be your ticket to success.

In other words, sometimes you'll want a fast, straight lure drop and a fast, straight retrieve, particularly when the water is deep and swift. For those times, a knife, potbelly or even standard diamond jig makes good sense, When you need more flutter and opportunity for a bite during the drop and a slower, erratic and enticing retrieve, perhaps when fishing mid and slower waters, a flutter-style jig can't be beat. It's all about the application. For some anglers and tackle shops, this new wave of specialty lures will be a passing fad. Other anglers, who study and really think about their fishing, will realize that certain methods of jigging are best suited for a particular day's fishing.

Unlike true diamond jigs, which have little variation among brands, deep-drop and flutter jigs are as varied as the fish they catch. While it's impossible to describe the entire dazzling array of new jigging lures on the market, let's review some of the current industry leaders.

Braid Metal Jigs

Braid tackle (http://braidproducts.com) offers numerous deep-drop and flutter-style metal jigs, such as their Tantrum Hammer jigs, which are available from 5½ to 7 ounces and in four colors. They come rigged with two assist Mustad 4x strong live-bait-style hooks. Some of Braid's other deep-drop lures include the Slim Swim and Super Deep jigs, which are elongated lures having excellent action on both the drop and the retrieve. The company also carries a wide variety—notably their 700 series and DB jig—of forward-weighted jigs, producing head-first dives when jigged. These jigs are normally fished with single or treble tail hooks.

Offshore Angler Freestyle Jig

Bass Pro Shops' Offshore Angler (www.basspro.com) offers their version of a flutter lure called the Freestyle jig. It's designed like other flutter jigs to have enticing action during both the drop and the retrieve while vertical jigging. The lures range in weight from 2 to 9 ounces. The Freestyle jig features a hologram finish, oversized 3-D eyes and a stainless-steel front split ring to which double Gamakatsu assist hooks are attached.

Offshore Angler also offers their Offshore Extreme Freestyle Jigging Trigger Rods designed specifically for use with flutter-style jigs and fine-diameter super braid line. These rods boast lightness, sensitivity and strength.

RIVER2SEA Knife Jigs

In about 2006, "knife" jigs arrived on the tackle scene. They derive their name from their knife-like profile. One of the knife-jig leaders is RIVER2SEA tackle (www.river2sea.com). Their Knife jig is designed to drop in deep waters without feeling too heavy and, according to RIVER2SEA, it's a good choice for light-tackle jig anglers. The knife jig's long, thin tail-heavy body plummets through the water column without tumbling and is ideal for deep yo-yo fishing for species like striped bass, cod, haddock, grouper and ling, among others. This lure's design makes it particularly effective in swift currents.

Shimano Butterfly Jigs

Shimano (www.shimano.com) introduced Butterfly jigs in the United States in 2005, and the company pioneered the development of an

Deep-drop and flutter-style jigs, such as the Shimano Butterfly Jig seen here, are very effective when combined with specific rod-and-reel action. Various styles of dangling assist hooks are standard on most jigs. Heavy-duty or wire tethers are important for toothy critters like bluefish.

entire deep-drop jigging system. This set-up consists of four basic components: Butterfly jigs, the Trevala jigging rod series with matching Shimano high-speed reels, loop-to-loop wind-on leaders and super braid line.

The action of the Butterfly jig results from its design. The sharp edges and angles of the flat surfaces help the jig cut through the water on both the fall and retrieve. It does not really flutter, according to Shimano, as do some similar jigs. Instead, the cutting action gives the jig an erratic swimming motion.

Shimano's Regular jig has a 3-D shape, which is heavier toward the tail than the front end. The Regular jig is four sided on its lower two-thirds and flatter near the front. This lopsided form helps the lure drop quickly but imparts a spiral, darting action during a vertical retrieve.

Shimano's Long jig features an asymmetrical 3-D body (narrow, long and six-sided) that offers horizontal action during the retrieve and a unique roll-wobble movement while falling. The offset center of gravity enables the jig to dart widely with every retrieve, thus creating an exaggerated horizontal presentation for mid-water fish.

The Flat-Side jig, Shimano's newest in the deep-drop line-up, is designed for the diagonal action needed when fishing from a fast-drifting boat. The rearward center of gravity allows the jig to fall with a swinging motion. An asymmetrical 3-D design on one side and flat-side mirror on the other side increases its action and appeal.

Shulure Vertical Jigs

The Shulure company (www.shulure.com) specializes in a series of five flutter and deep-drop vertical jigs. The Jigoon combines the features of a jig and spoon, giving the lure a smooth but erratic action allowing casting, jigging and trolling for a variety of game fish. The Long Bodied Vertical jig has a long profile producing a good flutter action on the drop and a fast yet erratic motion during the retrieve. The Medium Bodied Vertical jig is newly redesigned and has a thicker wider base, allowing it to drop more vertically but still have an erratic action on the retrieve. The Pencil Bodied jig is the thinnest of Shulure's vertical jigs and has good balance allowing a flutter action on the drop and enticing motion on the uptake. The last of Shulure's jigs, the Squish, has a unique, flattened profile combining the appearance of a squid and a baitfish. Glow-in-the dark finish helps predators find it in the depths.

Shulure's jigs are available in weights from 2 to 9 ounces and all come rigged with a single assist hook.

SPRO Sushi Spoon

SPRO (www.spro.com) has recently developed its own version of a deep-drop jig, called the Abalone Sushi Spoon. Not really a spoon at all, the lure looks similar to the other new deepwater jigs. SPRO wraps their Sushi Spoons in real abalone shell for brilliant, natural coloration. The obvious result is a higher costing, but pretty lure. Like other deep-drop and flutter jigs, the Sushi Spoon is designed for use with an assist hook rigged off the front eye. So far, the Sushi Spoon only comes in a 5-inch, 3-ounce model but in four color patterns. Anglers should fish this light jig by either squidding or yo-yo jigging in inshore rips.

Squid Jig Warehouse

Colman's Squid Jig Warehouse (www.squidjig.com), of Colman's Fishing Supply, carries a wide variety of lures imported directly from Asia that are suitable for vertical jigging. Two types, in particular, follow the design of deep-drop and flutter jigs called Laser Finish Metal Jigs. These laser-finish jigs feature a hard, smooth scratch-resistant surface.

One style is weighted slightly heavier towards the bottom, making it an excellent choice as a deep-water, fast-drop jig that will plummet tail-first. It's available in five holographic color patterns with a laser finish and protective, clear-epoxy coating. The finish also includes luminous glow-in-the-dark bellies, as do their other similar jigs. 3D-holographic eyes add to a realistic appearance. These vertical jigs are available in two sizes: a 5-ounce, 5-inch model and a 7-ounce 6-inch model. Unlike most other deep-drop lures, these come with treble hooks rigged off the tail, which is IGFA legal.

Squid Jig's second jig has the same finish qualities as their other Laser Finish jigs, but this one has a symmetrically-balanced squid shape. Its neutral center-of-gravity and equal taper at both ends provides the 6-inch, 5-ounce jig with an excellent flutter motion during the drop. This model comes without hooks, allowing the angler to use either a back-end J or treble hook and/or a leading assist-hook configuration.

Company owner, Jon P. Colman, has used the 24210-style jig along the Washington Coast for rockfish. He fishes them with treble hooks and sometimes adds a 4½-inch Octopus Skirt of various colors because it "gives the fish something to target." He fishes those with 50-pound braid line rigged to a 40-pound fluorocarbon leader. His 24208 model has been extremely popular in his California market, where the rear-attached treble is the favorite hook configuration. The lure is fished with a flutter drop within the bottom 20 feet of the water column.

Tormenter Chubby and Ribbonfish Jigs

Tormenter tackle (www.tormentertackle.com) has its own version of deep-drop and flutter jigs. The Chubby (7-inch, 9½-ounce), Chubby Jr. (5-inch, 5-ounce) and Chubby Mini (3½-inch, 3-ounce) are all tail weighted for deep water and heavy current applications. Tormenter's Large Ribbon Fish (14-inch, 14½-ounce) and Ribbon Fish (9-inch, 7½-ounce) are long, narrow, flat and neutrally-weighted flutter jigs created to "float" down like a wounded baitfish. Tormenter's Ballyhoo (4-inch, 3 ounce) is lead cast and painted but owes its flutter action to its flattened shape. Unlike their other two jigs, which are designed with a front assist hook in mind, the Ballyhoo come factory-rigged with a single 1.5X strong nickel-plated tail hook.

A different variation of the typical deep-drop lure, and unlike Tormenter's tail-heavy Chubby series, the Sardine is a head-weighted deep jig, so the head-end of the lure dives when you drop the rod tip and climbs when you raise it.

Dave Adams, founder and CEO of Tormenter Tackle, hit the market with his Chubby and Ribbonfish jigs at the same time as Shimano introduced its Butterfly jigs in the US. Adams, working in China with a company that produced many of the Japanese OEM tackle brands, says that Japan had tested and manufactured these lure styles for decades. Dave's first thought was to introduce deep-drop and flutter jigs to anglers using diamond jigs for cod in the Northeast. He started producing them in limited quantities, but increased production as the Butterfly-style lure craze suddenly caught on in this country.

Williamson Benthos and Abyss Speed Jigs

Williamson Lures (www.williamsonlures.com) offers two deep-drop jigs called the Benthos Speed jig and the Abyss Speed jig. Benthos means organisms living on, in or near the seabed, also known as the benthic zone, and Abyss means the greatest depths of the sea. A related term, abyssal plain, means the deep ocean basin floor. Clearly, Williamson is implying its are deep-fishing lures.

Williamson's Abyss jig features a potbelly shape (weighted toward the tail end), which enables the jig to drop fast. Its slender design has less retrieve resistance than other similar jigs, allowing the angler to fish harder and longer.

Steve Conn tuned his deep-drop Williamson Abyss jig for bluefish by adding a single Siwash hook on a swivel to the lure's tail end.

The somewhat diamond-shaped design of the Benthos jig allows it to drop fast vertically even in a strong current or during a fast drift. Glow-in-the-dark paint helps fish see the lure in deep, dark waters. Both the Benthos and Abyss Speed jigs are rigged with single assist hooks.

How to Fish Deep-Drop and Flutter Jigs

With flutter-style jigging, success is most often associated with the proper action you impart on the lure, rather than the jig's appearance. Fussy fish like tuna and stripers will often strike a flutter jig out of reaction or instinct, even if they aren't in a feeding mode.

Flutter-style jigging is a physically demanding type of fishing and one which can last all day. For this reason, experienced charter captains who specialize in jigging carry both conventional and spinning outfits. As you may know, spinning reels retrieve left-handed and conventional reels retrieve right-handed. Therefore, by using both types it's possible for anglers to switch off every hour to rest one arm and work the other. Keeping spinning outfits rigged and ready also allows for the quick casting of jigs to schools of breaking fish.

This system is made possible by a new wave of spinning reels, which has recently hit the market. Notable for their high-speed ratios, this generation of spinning tackle appears tailor-made for deep or extreme jigging. Heavy-duty frames and gearing coupled with more numerous drag washers let these reels hold up to the rigors of heavy jigs, great depths, strong fish and unforgiving braided line. These new reels, such as the Shimano Stella20000 and Daiwa Saltiga 6000 and 65000 are best matched with a 7-foot, medium-heavy- to heavy-action (depending on jig weight) rods with high-quality guides.

Aside from specific tackle, Shimano and several other companies recommend specialized fishing techniques for use of their flutter lures. One method of deep-drop jigging begins by free-spooling a lure to the desired depth—usually the bottom—with your rod tip pointing down. From that position, use one short lift of the rod tip with every turn of the handle repeated through the retrieve. In other words, lift the rod on the upward turn of the reel handle and drop the rod tip on the downward turn of the reel handle, your rod tip traveling only 10 to 20 inches depending on desired action and retrieve speed.

A second deep-drop technique consists of free-spooling your lure to the desired depth, then using one long lift of the rod tip, followed by slack line on the rod tip drop, reel in slack line and repeat until the jig reaches the desired height from the bottom. Free spool the lure and start again.

For flutter-style jigs the technique starts by free-spooling the lure to the desired depth—usually the bottom—with your rod tip pointing toward the water. Next, lift your rod tip with an upward snapping motion to the 11 o'clock position. Now drop your rod tip while reeling in slack, similar to when pumping your rod when fighting a big fish. When the line comes tight at the bottom of the rod drop repeat the snapping, dropping and reeling pattern until the jig reaches the desired height from the bottom. Free spool the lure and start again.

Shimano's Trevala rods and similar rods from other companies are specifically designed with a parabolic action to help add life to flutter jigs. Because these rods load with a quick turn of the reel handle, they then quickly release their stored energy to lift the jig upwards. Always use those rods rated for braided lines, and stay true to the manufacturer's recommendation for jig weights (foreign-made jigs are often labeled in grams). Otherwise, a parabolic rod will fish constantly bent and won't have the backbone to release its store energy to propel a heavier jig.

One of the advantages of flutter and deep-drop jigs is that many are made from metal alloys rather than pure lead. Certain alloys are heavier than lead and that, in combination with their shape, allows you to fish lighter flutter jigs than conventional diamond jigs and this often allows you to fish smaller jigs than conventional vertical jigs.

Super Deep Dropping

Another recent and important use for deep-drop jigs is, of course, true deep-drop fishing. Although deep-dropping or extreme jigging can and does include fishing for species like cod, haddock, rockfish, snapper and grouper in depths of 200 to 300 feet, the ultimate in deep-drop jigging occurs along the edge of the continental shelf, primarily for tilefish in the north and tilefish, ocean perch and grouper in the south. These marginally fishable waters, which span from New England to Key West and beyond, can range from 300 to 1,000 feet deep, but experts comfortably reach bottom with jigs in the 6- to 14-ounce range during the right conditions and by using super-braid line.

From the mid Atlantic northward, deep-drop pros spool 800 yards or more of 30- to 50-pound braid, often using the new breed of Butterfly-style jigging outfits such as a Shimano Trevalla rod and high-speed Torsa 20 reel, or a Penn Torque reel and Chaos jigging rod. In the south, however, experts like Capt. Ralph Delph, a pioneer in southern deep-drop jigging, spool their reels with super braid of less than 20-pound test, which allows them to fish in great depths with a minimum of line drag. Deep-drop fishermen routinely use 10 to 20 feet of wind-on mono or fluorocarbon leader in the 50- to 80-pound range.

Fishing with the thinnest main line possible allows the use of the lightest jigs possible, which also permits the use of light jigging outfits. This combination makes extreme jigging very sporting compared to traditional deep-drop bait-fishing techniques using cannonball lead weights, extra-heavy rods and electric reels for deep-ocean dwellers like golden and gray tilefish, snowy grouper, wreckfish and rosefish.

You must have a fast and seaworthy boat to make the long runs offshore to the drop-off (possibly 15 to 80 miles, depending on the region), and then you still must locate a likely spot, which isn't easy to do in a big ocean. Your best bet is to acquire some proven hot-spot numbers from a friend. If that's not possible, look for deep wrecks or areas marking plateaus right along the edge of the shelf, usually in waters of 600 to 800 feet deep. Or you can simply charter a captain specializing in this type of fishing.

Amazingly, as you drift over a likely area it may take three to seven minutes to reach bottom. Once your line stops, work the jig with a traditional yo-yo motion using long rod sweeps, letting the lure flutter on each drop. Depending on current speed and wind—both of which must be light—you may need to release line every few minutes to maintain the bottom. Tilefish and grouper often strike a jig as it flutters downward, so if your lure stops prematurely, set the hook. While grouper prefer structure, tilefish hang together in loose schools along clay bottoms (which they burrow into) so when you find one fish mark the spot with your electronics and repeat the drift because there will always be others.

To be fair, although the new-breed of deep-drop lures is ideal for this application, traditional diamond jigs—and even large bucktails— also work well in the hands of a pro. Some lure manufacturers also coat their jigs with glow paint, which helps attract fish in waters over 300 feet deep where little sunlight reaches.

Regardless of your jig choice, you'll likely increase your success by tipping jigs with a pork rind, soft-plastic tail or strip of sturdy bait such as squid, but keep the bait streamlined. If you simply skewer on a baitfish chunk, the added resistance will greatly reduce the speed of your jig's drop and you may never reach bottom. Big baits and slowly falling lures also increase your likelihood of hooking a shark.

Extreme jigging along "the edge" is also a great back-up plan when the offshore pelagic bite is off. Take a few suitable deep-jigging outfits with you the next time you run to the canyons and try some deep-dropping when the sun is high, the tuna have quit and the wind is calm. You may be pleasantly surprised at this untapped resource waiting along the shelf.

Ball Jigs

Ball jigs are another new wave of deep-water lures, which look like an elaborate fluke ball and perhaps represent a hybrid between a bucktail jig, a fluke ball and a deep-drop jig. The lures' overall appearance resembles that of a squid or octopus with trailing tentacles. They all have a large head shaped like a thick bullet or oblong globe with two large eyes. A silicon skirt and two squid-tentacle-like trailers are designed to flutter during jig movement. Two dancing assist-style hooks dangle from the body and hide in the skirt.

Braid Sea Fox and Thumper Jigs

Braid tackle offers new ball-type squid jigs called the Sea Fox and Thumper Squid jigs, which will fish in a variety of depths. These jigs have a heavy, round (Thumper Squid) or torpedo (Sea Fox) shaped head followed by a skirt with trailers and two dangling assist hooks.

Braid offers the Thumper Squid and Sea Fox jigs in eight weight sizes from ¾ ounce to 10½ ounces. Anglers can fish the Sea Fox jigs in three ways, depending on where the line is connected to the jig. According to Braid tackle, you can cast, troll or jig them for bottomfish. The Thumper Squid jigs are ideal for bottom-fishing applications, and the heaviest models are effective in depths up to 200 feet. The jigs are available in five colors patterns.

Shimano Lucanus Ball Jigs

The Lucanus Ball Jig differs greatly from their Butterfly jigs described above and the fishing theory behind Shimano's new lure is to catch sluggish, deepwater fish that might not usually strike a faster moving vertical jig. These jigs are available from 2 to 7 ounces.

The name Lucanus comes from *Lucanus cervus*, a type of stag beetle that lives in holes in old trees and dead trunks. (Once very common, the *Lucanus cervus* population, along with that of other species of beetles that feed on old wood, faces steep decline due to forest management practices and is now listed as globally threatened.)

Shimano, the creator of Butterfly jigs, decided to stay with the insect theme in naming its new lure. According to Shimano, the original Lucanus jig looked like a squid, but after many field tests they found that the jig worked better upside down. Viewing the Lucanus jig in that position, the lure looked more like a bug or beetle than a squid. The Lucanus jig is rigged with two swinging and trailing Owner hooks, which somewhat resemble the two jaws of the Lucanus cervus beetle.

The recommended technique to fish the Lucanus Ball Jig works this way: While your boat drifts in the current, free spool the jig to the bottom and then take seven or eight slow reel turns up. Free spool the ball jig again to the bottom, take seven or eight slow turns up and continue with this slow-motion squidding method until you have covered the desired area.

Once you feel a fish grab the tail of the lure, Shimano recommends you set the hook by continuous reeling, as you would a circle hook, rather than sharply lifting the rod tip: "Do not set the hook at the initial bites; keep reeling until the fish hooks itself. Once you feel the weight of the fish on the lure, then lift the rod to make sure the hooks are set firmly."

Although the Lucanus, Sea Fox and Thumper Squid are primarily designed for vertical jigging, these new jigs would probably make excellent weighted lures at the bottom of a three-way rig, replacing the standard bucktail when drifting for fluke.

IGFA Assist Hook Rules

Anglers who fish in hopes of an International Game Fish Association (IGFA) record must rig dangling assist hooks properly to avoid disqualification. According to IGFA rules, which are designed to prevent intentional foul-hooking, the distance between the end of the lure and a trailing hook's eye cannot exceed the hook's length. That means the legality of a jig depends on the lure's length, the length of the assist-hook leader (measured from end loop to hook bend) and where it attaches to the lure.

For example, if a jig measures 6 inches long and the assist-hook leader measures 7 inches, the lure would only be legal if the assist hook is attached to the front of the lure, as is typical with factory-rigged flutter and deep-drop jigs. However, if you remove even a fairly short hook-and-tether rig from the front of the jig and attach it to the tail of the jig it would place the trailing hook's eye more than one hook length behind the lure and violate IGFA rules, thereby disqualifying your prize catch.

Dangling assist hooks are effective for predators like striped bass that strike at the head of prey, as Jake Snell shows here.

Another regulation sometimes needing clarification concerns a vertical (deep-drop, flutter or diamond) jig with a treble hook attached to its back end and a single, dangling assist hook or two attached to its front end. Those configurations are permissible (Rule H.2). The IGFA ruling is that treble hooks are allowed if affixed directly to the tail-end of the hook, including via a split ring or a barrel swivel, but a vertical jig may not have a tethered "stinger" treble hook trailing from the back end of the lure as per the statement above. The IGFA permits a maximum of two single, dangling assist hooks from the front of a jig with the options of a single, a treble or no hook attached directly to a jig's back end.

18

SPECIAL USES—FLY FISHING
COMBO AND SABIKI RIGS

Combination Fly Fishing and Diamond Jigging

Like most other fish, bluefish often feed in schools. This schooling tendency creates competition for food within the group, and like gulls fighting over a fish carcass, predatory bluefish will chase down forage that a schoolmate is pursuing. Being extremely aggressive, they'll even swipe at a baitfish or lure in another blue's mouth. Fly fishermen can use this competitive behavior to their advantage when blues are feeding too deep to reach with flies.

The concept behind tag-team or buddy fishing is that one angler using diamond jigging gear draws bluefish within reach of a fly caster by hooking a fish near the bottom and cranking it up to the top. The fly fisherman stands on lookout—best accomplished from a higher vantage point such as a bow platform—with fly rod ready to cast to any free-swimming "buddy" fish following the hooked fish to the surface.

For those of you who've always wanted to try sight casting, but have had nowhere to do it, tag-team fishing offers the chance to spot and cast to individual fish. And, if you're a novice fly caster, tag-teaming lets you use fly gear without making long casts to reach the fish.

Fly-fishers usually pass by deeper reefs believing the waters are unfishable. The reason, of course, is the difficulty in dropping a fly far enough, fast enough in the strong tidal water, which can be 20 to 35 or more feet deep. Even the fastest sinking line is usually useless in these conditions.

If you don't know of any rips in your area, ask at a local tackle shop or check a chart for spots where the depth rises abruptly. Look for reefs or shoals running perpendicular or diagonal to the current flow. Typically, productive structure in areas like Long Island Sound bulge from a mud or sand bottom of about 50 to 60 feet to only 15 to 35 feet. In my experience, buddy bluefish seldom follow a hooked competitor

Al Buchman, left, and Mike Kai teamed up with a conventional outfit and diamond jig to draw this buddy bluefish within easy casting range of a fly.

all the way to the surface from reefs deeper than 35 feet, so it's probably pointless to try this technique in very deep areas.

Because buddy fish are attracted to a large, bright jig in their schoolmate's mouth, your fly should roughly fit that description. Tag-team fish don't need convincing—they're already in a feeding mood. Many patterns will produce heart-stopping strikes right next to the boat. Examples of good choices are large, bright Clousers and Deceivers tied on 3/0 hooks.

The Deceiver/Clouser pattern known as the Half-and-Half in chartreuse, red and white is an ideal fly choice. The bright green and tinsel are favorites for attracting bluefish, while the red imitates a bleeding baitfish. The weight of a Clouser's metal eyes helps it sink faster, which is important with this tag-team technique.

The best conditions for the angler are sunny days with light winds of 5 to 10 knots to create a ripple on the water's surface because you can still see the buddy fish, but they can't see you as well and so have fewer tendencies to spook.

Another advantage of this technique is that you can accomplish it on very windy days. In a seaworthy boat it's still possible to fish within a mile of shore when the winds are blowing offshore at 25 knots. Normal distance fly casting would be nearly impossible under those conditions.

After selecting a likely rip, work the jig with a typical squidding retrieve. As soon as a fish is hooked, however, you need to involve the flycaster as soon as possible. Quickly work the bluefish to the top to keep any buddy fish in close pursuit. It's important, if possible, to prevent the hooked fish from thrashing on the surface or jumping because that may scare off any followers. Polarized sunglasses are extremely helpful to spot free-swimmers, and they also protect the eyes from wind-blown flies.

Once a buddy fish is sighted, keep the hooked fish on the conventional line while the other angler quickly casts a fly in front of the free swimmer—you won't have much time before he disappears, and avoid slapping the surface with the fly line. Retrieve the fly like an injured baitfish. Stripping baskets, while preferred by many saltwater flycasters, aren't needed because casts are so short. When a bluefish strikes set the hook firmly by stripping, not by lifting the rod. Then hold on!

A 9-foot, 9-weight fly rod is a good choice. You won't be making long casts, but you'll also want some backbone. Match the rod to a deep-spool reel capable of handling a 9-weight line and 150 to 200 yards of 20- to 30-pound Dacron backing. Preferred line choices are an intermediate- or fast-sink, weight-forward line. I like clear fly line because it lessens chances of spooking fish near the boat. Even if the free swimmer ghosts into the depths and you lose sight of it, keep working your fly down deep because they're often suspended in the water column looking up for leftover baitfish morsels.

Use short fly leaders for fast, accurate presentations. A non-tapered, four-foot, 25-pound-test fluorocarbon leader is all you need. A short, dark, wire bite tippet at the fly is a must to avoid cut-offs from bluefish.

Sabiki Rigs

You can use sabiki rigs in tandem with diamond jigs to improve hookup rates for baitfish and game fish. A sabiki rig is a monofilament leader several feet long with a series of four to seven small hooks tied along its length. Hook sizes can range from tiny 14 to 1/0. Rigs vary in length depending on the number of hooks, but usually 10 inches of leader spans between 4-inch-long droppers with a hook on each. Swivels are attached to both ends of the rig.

The hooks are similar to saltwater flies and may be dressed with any combination of bucktail, nylon, feathers or plastic tubing or skirts, but they are usually fished unbaited. The purpose of a sabiki

This angler aboard the *Watch Out* uses a sabiki rig weighted with a diamond jig to catch four baitfish at one time for the live well. *Photo by Capt. Ned Kittredge.*

or mackerel rig is to catch numerous small baitfish at one time, such as mackerel, herring, shad or small jacks. Sabiki rigs are extremely light and must be weighted at the end to carry the flies to the appropriate depth where the schools are holding. The most common weight option is to use a sinker of a few ounces, but attaching a small diamond jig to the end of the leader has a duel function—it carries the rig quickly to the appropriate depth, and it adds the chance of catching one more baitfish or even a predator—on the jig.

The trick to catching baitfish is finding them. Your best bets are to obtain recent fishing reports, keep a close eye on your depthfinder or watch for surface action as you cruise in likely areas such as rips or bays. Once you locate fish, position your boat over the school and vertically jig a sabiki rig through them using a yo-yo motion with medium spinning or conventional tackle. You can buy these rigs at tackle stores, through catalogs, on line or you can make your own, which is a fun winter project. Use care when storing and transporting sabiki rigs, however, to avoid nasty tangles.

III

Fishing Bucktail Jigs

19

HOW TO RIG AND TUNE BUCKTAILS

Rigging bucktail jigs is not complicated. Most anglers use a basic clinch knot to tie their leader to the eye of the jig head. A superior knot, which is also easy to tie, is a Palomar. Its main benefits are that it doesn't slip, and it places a double line around the jig eye for more strength. For optimum lure action, southern anglers usually use a non-slip loop knot.

Leaders usually range from 18 to 24 inches in length and fluorocarbon is usually preferred because anglers traditionally fish bucktail jigs in shallow, bright water where monofilament is easier to see. You can secure your main line to the leader in several ways, including line to line knots or by using a swivel or snap-swivel.

One of the few drawbacks to using natural-hair bucktail jigs is that the fibers become damaged, causing them to break or pull out from the head, especially when catching toothy critters like Spanish mackerel, barracuda and bluefish. Bucktail jigs are costly enough that there's no sense discarding tired jigs to purchase new ones. Plus, of course, the lead head should be recycled. You can do this by replacing the bucktail hair yourself.

The equipment and materials you'll need include a small workbench vise, a bobbin (the thread holder fly tiers use), heavy duty thread (carpet thread works well for the larger jigs), clear fingernail polish, a white deer tail, a colored deer tail or colored synthetic fibers (available where fly tying material are sold) and small cans or bottles of oil-based enamel paint (model paint will work).

First, place your jig hook securely in the vise, being sure to clamp it on the bend of the hook rather than pinching the barb and point, which may cause the tip to lose its tensile strength. Next, you need to get rid of the old material on the lead head. Do this by slicing off the hair and thread with a single-edge razor blade, being sure to remove everything right down to the bare lead neck. With your bobbin, wrap the neck with a layer of thread to form a non-slip base for the hair. When you're finished, just let the bobbin hang, and do not cut the thread.

Your next step is to select a narrow tuft of hair from the underside base of the white (natural) deer tail. However, if you are creating a jig intended for night fishing, you should use the dark brown or black hair from the top of the tail.

If you have no background in fly tying, selecting the proper deer tail has more science to it than you might think. Proper hair choice is especially important when repairing smaller jigs. Some tails offer straight hairs, which make them perfect for narrow baitfish imitations like silversides, sand eels or American eels. On the other hand, some tails offer wavy hairs, which are well suited for creating fuller and wider bucktails imitating thicker baitfish like bunker or squid, because the kinks provide more space between the fibers.

Deer tail hair texture varies, too. Softer hairs are much easier to tie onto a lead head, and they flow gracefully and naturally when retrieved. Coarse, thicker hairs are more difficult to work with and attach; however, some large, deep water jigs may perform better with a mop-like appearance and action.

If looking at a deer tail and visualizing it in three equal parts from top (outside) to bottom (underside), you'll find the softer and finer hair near the top. The longer but still soft hairs appear at the mid section. The longest and thickest hairs are anchored at the base. Tails also vary from one animal to another. Some may exhibit an area of very thick, coarse hair all the way to the bottom. The main characteristic of these hairs is that they will flare when tied tightly with thread, which would give them better pulsing action.

Once you have selected the type of hair you desire and grasped a tuft, cut it at its base with a pair of small, sharp scissors. Next, pinch the long guard hairs firmly in the middle of the free tuft and use your other hand to thin out or groom any short base hairs. Trim the butt end, if necessary, to be sure all the hairs are even. However, never cut the tapered end.

Place the cut end of the tuft against the base of the lead head and secure it to the hook shank with a few firm wraps of the thread. Repeat this process several times until you have laid the desired volume of hair around the entire base of the neck, being sure to tie the hairs in parallel to the shank and not on a diagonal. You don't need excessive amount of hair, and you should avoid over-packing it. A bucktail jig with too much hair will look and act like a wet mop, and there's a high likelihood that the hairs will pull out after the first fish grabs the lure.

Once you're satisfied with the hair surrounding the entire hook shank, take some extra wraps around the hair to secure it firmly to the jig's neck. At this point, you can now add some synthetic or natural-color fibers to the jig to create your preferred color pattern. Black, red, pink, blue or chartreuse are popular jig hair colors and would work well. You can place this small cluster of colored fibers along the hook shank as you desire, with the final result to look like a racing stripe down the belly or back of the white deer hair.

Use your bobbin to lay down enough additional thread wraps around the jig neck area to build up a level and solid thread surface. If you know how to tie a whip finish, use that knot to secure the thread and then cut it. If not, use a few half hitches. Apply the clear nail polish (exterior or marine polyurethane applied with an artist's brush will also work) so it evenly coats the thread on all sides. Do not apply too thickly, but rather let dry and apply two more coats, being sure not to let it sag and dry.

Last, if you like, you can repaint the lead head and then let it dry. Later, use red paint and a pointed artist's brush to add red eyes, mouth and gills. If you want to pour your own lead to make new bucktails, a wide variety of jig molds are available from Do-It Molds at www.do-it-molds.com. These molds cost about $40.00 each in a tackle shop.

A before-and-after comparison shows two examples of what a lead-head and fixed-hook jig looks like before deer tail hair and enamel paint are applied. With a small workbench vice and some basic fly-tying materials you can easily tune-up your old bucktail jigs. The finished jig in the middle is 3-ounce model made by Spro. *Photo by Maggie Migdalski.*

20

NEARSHORE, SHALLOWS AND FLATS

Bucktails are popular with beach fishermen, those anglers actually standing in the sand or on rock jetties, however, this book only discusses fishing from boats, so in this section I will review a few "surf" strategies for boaters.

If you choose to cast bucktails toward clear beaches (those lacking structure), you should target areas where slopes are most prominent. On these types of open beaches, the few variables are water depth and any shoreline contours. Many sand beaches fade into mixed or rocky bottoms below the low-tide line, and that's another likely staging spot for predators.

Unlike shore-bound anglers who strive to cast as far as possible, boat fishermen aren't as concerned with distance because they only need to move their boat to reach the desired area. Therefore, you can use lighter jigs and shorter rods than do shore casters. The lightest jig you'll probably use is about ⅜ to 1 ounce, which is good for clear, shallow water and when the local baitfish are small. Moving up to 1½ to 2 ounces allows you to cover more water faster and deeper water, maintaining a tighter line and hopping your jig down the slopes away from the beach. It's this shelf or transition zone, often fading to the rocky patches, where you find predators waiting to ambush prey. Save jigs larger than 2 ounces for working deep water with fast currents like passes and channels, which is covered in a following chapter.

Using a medium-action spinning outfit of 7 to 7½ feet, cast the bucktail to the surf line, allow it to sink to the bottom and retrieve it on or near the bottom using sharp, short rod-tip lifts with every four to five turns of the reel handle. Maintain a tight line, especially as your jig falls, because strikes can be subtle and often occur on the drop. Fluorocarbon leaders help fool keen-eyed fish in clear, shallow surfs.

When you're faced with uneven sized, closely packed rocks covered by shallow water (10 to 20 feet deep) use a jetty caster-style bucktail of about 1 ounce. The idea is for the jig to be light enough to run over the highest rocks, keeping the bucktail from making more than just occasional contact on the tops of the boulders, rather than dropping it between them and causing snags, but be sure the hook is of sufficient size to handle the predators you expect in this type of structure.

In areas where boulders are few and dispersed, you need to drop your lure down between them. You'll risk losing a few jigs, assuming they are heavy enough to drop between the big rocks, but that's the gamble you must take. After fishing an area a few times, you'll learn where the boulders are, and you'll be able to fish around them more precisely to avoid losing rigs. Carry tackle, line and leader heavy enough to pull big fish from these areas.

Structure can be located in any depth of water. While reefs, banks, shoals and wrecks make up most of the offshore diamond jigging hotspots, nearshore structure like boulders, small islands, keys, bridge abutments, piers and dock pilings can all create or block turbulence. These obstacles are always good spots to work bucktails.

Casting small bucktails to structure like docks and piers is a great way to draw snook out of the shadows, as Carol Migdalski and Capt. Ralph Allen did in southwest Florida.

Dead spots are areas where the current is weaker than in the surrounding water and often hold predators. A dead spot can occur behind any object that obstructs water flow—a good example is a boulder cluster in a tidal river, such as occurs in the lower Connecticut River in southeastern Connecticut. However, the sweet spot effect also occurs immediately in front of these obstacles because oncoming water piles up against the structure and counters the current. Predators hold near the bottom in both these small sheltered areas to conserve energy and wait for baitfish or other forage to drift past.

Breakwaters, jetties, bars, tombolos and canal corners also offer good fishing as the current courses along, around or over them. They hinder baitfish escape routes, yet the forage is attracted by the structure and accumulates there in the sheltered areas.

Common knowledge among fishermen, especially for shallow, southern waters like Charlotte Harbor in southwest Florida, is that small baitfish accumulate on the windward side of landmasses. Established reasoning and belief says this phenomenon happens because the baits are "blown" downwind and pushed against the shores.

Bob Skoronski fights a big redfish hooked on a bucktail in the shallows of Charlotte Harbor, Florida, as Capt. Dan Latham, on Bob's left, looks on.

But Capt. Ralph Allen, a longtime shallow-water expert in Punta Gorda, Florida, doesn't agree with that explanation. He feels the wind effect in bays and harbors is minimal underwater, and baitfish could easily swim against it. Rather, he believes bunches of small particles—like plankton, tiny crustaceans, fish eggs, and other microscopic foods—are blown against the shore and they, in turn, draw the small baitfish to feed on the forage.

Whatever the reason, baitfish do gather on the windward side of shores, as do the predators that feed on them. On windy days, novices seek the sheltered side of islands or keys, but experts anchor on the windward side and cast their small bucktails to the windblown shoreline.

Good fishing also occurs if you cast or drift your bucktails in front of and along the ends of formations where the tide sweeps past. Don't overlook cuts, pockets, bowls, spits and other bulges or depressions in shorelines having strong tidal flow. During slow current periods, or when fishing the shallow water on top of bars or slopes, try casting small bucktails like a 1¼-ounce rip splitter-style and hop it along the bottom and back to your anchored or drifting boat using a medium-light spinning or baitcasting outfit.

Shoreline waters are almost always less than 8 feet deep, and baitfish are almost always present. That's because thin water in bays and estuaries is one of the few areas where baitfish can safely swim without fearing predators, especially at low tide when they disperse over the flats. As the tide rises, however, gamefish move in and baitfish are pushed tighter against the shore. Two hours on either side of high tide offers bucktail fishermen a narrow band of water along the shoreline where predators and prey are present and concentrated.

If possible, plan your trips around the times of high tide and when a gentle wind is blowing parallel to the coast. That allows you to motor within casting range of the bait zone, cut the engine and drift parallel to shore. This technique offers a stealthy approach while covering lots of territory. When you catch a fish, note your position against a shoreline feature or drop a retrievable, anchored float so you can repeat successful drifts.

Always use the slowest retrieve that conditions allow and without digging the nose of the jig into the mud or sand. Ideally, you want a jig to hop or swim within about two feet of the bottom, which is where most shoreline predators prowl. When the tide reaches its lower stages, your best strategy then is to switch to a lighter jig— perhaps a bucktail having a half-ounce head—and increase your casting area and retrieve rate. If you are drifting over a clear bottom of 8

Carol Migdalski hooked this large snook on a bucktail and horsed it from the mangroves aboard Capt. Ralph Allen's flats boat in southwest Florida.

feet or deeper, you can also "double-dip" by casting a bucktail toward the shore with one rod while drifting a second rod and jig (tipped with fresh bait) on the bottom for flatfish.

Whether points occur off an island or the mainland they're particularly good fishing spots. They attract predators because forage is concentrated and forced around their ends in the enhanced currents they create. Fishing in these areas usually requires bucktails at least a ½ ounce heavier than you would use in similar depth and bottom conditions without the strong current. You may also need to upgrade to slightly heavier tackle to accommodate the heavier jigs and line needed around any structure.

A heavier bucktail allows you to cover water more accurately with a tighter line while keeping your jig along the bottom as you drift around a point. The additional weight is important when species like stripers, weakfish, flatfish, snook or sea trout hold close to the bottom to escape the current and wait for prey.

In southern waters, shoreline structure also comes in the form of overhanging mangroves. Around the times of high tide, quietly work your boat to within casting distance of the trees and toss a small bucktail as close to the roots as possible, which may mean occasionally snagging your lure in the branches. During the two hours on either side of high tide, predators like snook chase baitfish well under the overhanging branches, and you're not likely to get a strike unless you risk casting into their feeding zone. With practice, you'll be able to side-arm cast a small jig directly under the branches. This fishing, however, requires heavier tackle and line to muscle big fish out from the structure, but don't overlook sand holes or channels in the flats. When you come across such depressions, cast you jig across them and hop it across the bottom, which is a great way to pick up large fish during hot or bright conditions.

Your best strategy for fishing on flats or in shallows without structure or depressions is to try to see the fish before you cast to them. Professional guides have a well-honed ability to spot fish ghosting over the flats, but with some practice you'll be able to distinguish them against varied bottoms. Look for wakes from cruising fish, fins or tails breaking the surface or scattering baitfish.

As you are likely aware, the most common method of stalking flats fish from a boat is tipping up your main motor and then poling or using an electric motor to move within range of fish. In some hotspots up north, such as windy Nantucket Island, a common method is to run your boat upwind (or uptide) of a promising stretch of water, then cut the motor and drift, assisted by poling if necessary, while searching the thin water for the telltale dark forms. A high vantage point, such as a poling platform or bow cover, is helpful in locating fish, as are polarized sunglasses and a visor cap.

According to Capt. Hal Herrick, a longtime guide on Nantucket, spotting the fish and accurate casting are both very important. When working the shallows for stripers he advises looking for dark, shadowy forms moving against the current—especially watching the lighter sand areas between the darker weed and rock patches.

Using a light jig that won't create a big plop when it lands, cast your lure slightly in front of a fish's path. But you must first judge the fish's speed to accurately gauge the distance to lead it by. Never just plunk a bucktail in the middle of a pod because the fish will scatter and vanish. Instead, cast to the perimeter of the school and retrieve your jig across or away from the group like escaping prey, but never retrieve it towards them. After all, a baitfish about to become a predator's next meal would never swim toward the danger.

Work your jig with small, quick bounces, imitating the forage living in that habitat. If you can't spot any predators, fan the area by using long, arching casts and work your jig back with momentary pauses between each rod tip lift. If you venture into deeper water, perhaps 4

Redfish are a viable target for bucktail fishermen. Capt. Dan Latham boated this beauty after hopping a bucktail through a hole in the back-country of Florida's Charlotte Harbor.

feet deep or more, you may need to switch to a heavier jig. Change your technique as well by lifting your rod tip higher for bigger jig hops. If you locate baitfish schools, especially those worked by predators, reel the jig faster to keep it suspended and swimming rather than bumping the bottom and hopping, thereby more closely simulating the baitfish.

A good, all-around choice for a shallow-water leader is 18 inches of 30-pound fluorocarbon tied to the main line with a uni-knot. But you can drop as low as 20-pound leader for fussy targets like redfish and striped bass or go as high as 40-pound leader for species like snook and big stripers because of their sandpapery mouths and sharp gill plates. If you anticipate bluefish, come prepared with some wire bite tippet or risk losing a lot of jigs.

For shallows, whether in the north or south, a good outfit is a 7½-foot rod capable of handling 8- to 17-pound-class line and rigged 15-pound super braid. Super braids work well for these applications because they are very strong for their diameter, cast well, take a lot of abuse around structure and don't kink on a spinning reel. Many anglers tip their shallow-water bucktails with pork rind or soft plastic tails, which enhance the action and attractiveness of jigs.

21

INLETS, PASSES AND RIPS

Inlets, passes, river mouths and large canals are other fish-gathering hotspots that are much more practical to work with bucktails instead of with diamond jigs. They can range from tidal openings between landmasses such as barrier islands or keys to big rivers of fast-flowing water colliding with a gulf or ocean.

Characteristically, most inlets and passes have a main channel running along their length and sandbars at their mouth. Large and numerous fish stage in these cuts, primarily in the center of the channel or along channel edges. Such spots are often challenging to fish due to current, depth, waves or weekend boat traffic, but they also give you an opportunity for a prize like a large flatfish, striped bass, redfish, snook or tarpon.

The best seasons to target inlets and passes are during peak migration periods such as spring and fall when predators are moving into or out of an area. In the Northeast, for example, summers are usually slow times for inlets because fish like striped bass and weakfish are staging out on the deeper reefs. One exception is at night, when gamefish may follow baitfish, like menhaden, into the bays and harbors.

If you plan to fish at night, be sure of your navigational abilities and electronics and always leave your boat lights on. Also, switch jig color from daytime's standard white to black or purple-and-black bucktails tipped with black pork rind. Black offers a much better silhouette at night. All other daytime fishing strategies remain the same at night.

Keep in mind that narrow inlets generally carry very strong currents and turbulence due to the large amount of water being forced through a constricted area. Although exceptions always exist, the opposite is also true: The wider the inlet the gentler the current flow. Watch the forecast for winds that may oppose an outgoing current

Although rips, passes and inlets can be treacherous to navigate, during the right conditions they are an excellent places to drift bucktails for big fish. Predators almost always favor the up-tide side of structure.

because they can create treacherous seas at the entrance. Generally speaking, you need to increase your bucktail and tackle size as well as change your casting technique when working inlets, passes and similar areas.

When plying hotspots like the Cape Cod Canal or the Boca Grande Pass during peak tides, especially during full moon conditions with an opposing wind, you should come prepared to drift or cast big bucktails. An example of such a jig is the Andrus Big-Eye of 4 to 6 ounces, which is designed and marketed for these environments. You should still always use the lightest weight bucktail possible for the conditions. In shallower or slower channels and passes, 2- to 3-ounce bucktails should perform well, but fishing during slack water isn't the answer to heavy jigs because predators seldom feed during slack tide.

In situations where you are anchored in a current near a channel, use different length casts. Start by making short tosses up current, targeting the slope and using a hopping motion during a slow retrieve. After covering the closest area, use increasingly long uptide casts aimed to fall deeper into the channel. The purpose of casting diagonally uptide is so your jig reaches bottom before sweeping down current. Once the lure passes a point diagonally downtide of you (in other words, if you are anchored into the current, this spot is about a 135-degree angle from the bow) the water force sweeps the lure behind the boat, taking it out of the strike zone and robbing it of its natural drifting action.

Casting downtide is usually a waste of time. Retrieving your bucktail against a strong current ruins its action and creates an unrealistic appearance. Most baitfish and other forage like shrimp and crabs can't or won't fight a strong current, and they almost always travel with or across the flow. Therefore, whenever your jig passes that downtide diagonal position, just crank it in fast and make a new cast.

After casting uptide, your line will go slack when your jig reaches bottom. Retrieve it with long, steady pulls of the rod, thereby imitating struggling baitfish like herring, shad, menhaden or mullet. If that action doesn't trigger strikes, try hopping your bucktail along the bottom with short, quick rod-tip lifts. Always keep your line tight on the drop because predators often strike jigs on the fall, and if your line is slack you may not detect a subtle pick-up. When you feel a strike, reel quickly until your rod loads and firmly set the hook. Super braid lines in the 20- to 50-pound range are good choices for detecting strikes and reducing water drag with heavy bucktails in these massive conveyer-belts of water.

Always look for any structure that will break the full force of the current, such as a driftwood tree trunk, old dock pilings, sandbar or boulder field, where fish can conserve energy watching and waiting for passing food. Focus your casts or drifts to take your lure along the front, back and ends of any such obstructions, being careful to avoid hitting your engine's lower unit. Another strategy is to start above structure or riffled water caused by submerged structure, and then work your way downcurrent until you are back in flat water.

Almost any bucktail substantial enough to reach bottom, usually tipped with a strip of squid, pork rind or soft-plastic tail, is an excellent lure to cast or drift in big-water locations. Match your tackle to the conditions and lure weight, starting with a medium-action spin or baitcasting outfit and moving up from there. Retrieve your big bucktail using short hopping motions with the rod tip along structure edges. Fluorocarbon is only necessary in areas clear or shallow enough to permit a lot of sunlight.

When the current decreases, especially on a dropping tide, predators cruise out from the protection of nearshore structure or slopes and settle into the deep channels. Their movement allows you to fan cast or drift in more general areas of the waterway, especially searching out any holes, depressions or basins. Be prepared to switch to heavier jigs, and possibly heavier tackle, when moving from shoreline features to the depths of channels or passes.

Ed Maturo hooked this striped bass by working a bucktail up the face of a reef in western Long Island Sound.

You can fish rips by anchoring, by slowly motoring diagonally against the tide, called stemming the tide, or by drifting. If fish are driving bait to the surface along a rip, run your boat to within casting distance, kill the engine and cast to the breaking pod while drifting toward the rip line. Try letting your jig sink below the school and then jigging it up through it using a combination of rod-tip lifts and reeling action. Predators engaged in feeding frenzies don't need much convincing, so your presentation doesn't need to be perfect. If the predators have sharp teeth like bluefish, be sure to use a 6-inch wire bite-leader, but don't expect your jig's body material to last too long.

If your targets are breaking bonito or false albacore, tie on a small, white, bullet-head bucktail (without a pork rind or soft-plastic tail trailer) and cast it across and in front of the action. Retrieve it immediately with fast reel turns and short rod-tip twitches. These fish have great eyesight; therefore, use an 18-inch fluorocarbon leader of only 20-pound-test attached to a spool of 15-pound hybrid mono, like Yo-Zuri's mono with its hard outer layer and flexible inner core, via a small, black 35-pound snap-swivel or a uni-knot-to-uni-knot connection.

Stemming the tide is easier with two people onboard—one to cast and one to jockey the boat ahead of the rip and keep it in place by

As this big bluefish proves, striped bass aren't the only Northeast predator that likes bucktails tipped with a pork rind and worked in front of nearshore rips.

constantly adjusting the throttle. This can be tricky for both people if the rip is strong. The stern is the best place for the fisherman to stand and cast, but be sure the craft is seaworthy enough to drift into a rip line stern first. You'll need heavier tackle for these conditions and jigs of at least 4 ounces with heavy leader. Cast diagonally uptide and work you jig back to the boat, as described earlier.

Drifting, however, is the easiest approach. Start your drift well ahead of the rip line and bounce your jig vertically and yo-yo style along the bottom until you have cleared the reef and worked down the back side. Once again, a strip of squid, pork rind or a soft-plastic tail greatly enhances the jig's appeal.

Pay attention to where you catch fish on each reef. Then use triangulation, electronics or an anchored float, like an empty bleach bottle tied to a brick, to return to that exact spot on successive passes. Fighting and landing a big fish in a strong rip requires skill by both angler and helmsman, and your craft should be seaworthy enough to handle the rip if you need to drift into it to play a big fish like a striped bass.

If you choose to cast rather than free-spool vertically in areas where there are drastic rises and drops in the bottom contour, keep your casting distances short to avoid snags. Focus on the structure immediately around you while drifting or anchored. Boulder fields and reefs composed of bedrock have jagged vertical relief. The current will help your jig dance enticingly as it's worked over the structure, but keep the lure close to home and simply move the boat to cover other areas.

White is your best all-purpose choice for bucktails. North or south, east or west, you can't go wrong with white. Exceptions to this rule occur when no baitfish or squid are available and species like striped bass or redfish must revert to feeding on crustaceans like shrimp, crabs, mantis shrimp and baby lobsters. In those cases, imitating the size and color of the predominant shellfish is your best bet. Try white first, tipping it with a white or white-over-red pork rind, choosing the size of the pork rind to match the size of the jig. The other exception is night, and that's when you should switch to black or dark purple to create better silhouettes for predators to see.

22

OFFSHORE—SOUTH COAST

Although diamond jigging is much less common in southern waters, fishing with bucktails is very popular along the southeast coast and in the Gulf of Mexico. Along Florida's west coast, for example, gag grouper are prime targets for vertical jigging in depths of approximately 30 to 100 feet, which may require running many miles offshore to reach.

According to Capt. Ralph Allen, owner of the *King Fisher* fleet in Punta Gorda, Florida, gag grouper congregate around small rock ledges and outcroppings offering 2 to 4 feet of vertical relief on an otherwise flat bottom. Because these ledges may only run 50 feet or fewer in length, precise boat positioning is critical for success. Veteran bottom bouncers like Capt. Allen anchor slightly upcurrent of the structure and then tap their jig along the bottom, attempting to either work it parallel to the edge of the ledge or to hop it on top until it drops over the edge into deeper water.

Grouper strike with force, often inhaling a bucktail and immediately dashing to the safety of the ledge or artificial reef where they try to escape capture by boring as far back beneath the structure as possible. Experienced anglers apply maximum pull on the rod as soon as they feel a strike, straining the tackle to almost the breaking point in an attempt to stop the fish from reaching the protection of the overhang.

Jig fishermen also target red grouper in the Gulf, but those fish aren't quite as aggressive at taking artificials as are gag grouper. Reds also scatter more across Swiss cheese-type bottoms, which is a habitat created by relatively flat sheets of limestone pocked by round or oval holes, similar in appearance to a piece of Swiss cheese lying on a table. Since this type of bottom is much more expansive than the small ledges favored by gag grouper, it's possible to catch red grouper from a drifting boat. This is the most efficient way to cover ground

Capt. Steve Skevington shows a grouper he jigged up over rugged bottom about 25 miles off the coast of southwest Florida in the Gulf of Mexico.

and locate fish scattered over a wide area. Reds are attracted to their prey by scent as well as sight; therefore, many jig anglers sweeten their lures with strips of squid or bonito bellies or even a live bait like a blue runner or pinfish. Some fishermen also use artificial baits such as Berkley Gulp! or Fishbites.

Bucktail choices range from as little as 1 ounce on up to 4 ounces depending on water depth and current speed. Most anglers prefer egg-shaped jig heads, though some swear by flattened jig heads because they flutter more on the drop. Head colors are usually white or red, and bodies are commonly white, yellow or chartreuse, although every color has its proponents.

Light tackle isn't practical for halting big grouper headed for hiding holes. Grouper anglers fish with a minimum of 30-pound-test line, and some will use lines as strong as 80- to 100-pound. The new breed of super braid lines offer the advantage of low stretch—better to put the brakes on a fleeing fish—and more sensitivity for feeling bites in deep water. Some anglers, however, still prefer monofilament line because the braids can create difficult tangles—especially on charter boats—and improperly loaded braided lines may dig into the spool when under heavy pressure.

Another expert in Gulf Coast jig fishing is Capt. Steve Skevington, who runs Paradise Fishing Charters off Ft. Myers Beach, Florida. Capt. Skevington uses 3-ounce yellow bucktails for permit hovering over Gulf wrecks, which are located starting at about 10 miles offshore in 25-foot depths to as far as 40 miles offshore in depths up to 110 feet. In situations like this, let the jig fall to the depth the fish are holding, which could be anywhere from 5 to 90 feet deep, work the jig back to the boat with short jerks of the rod tip in an effort to simulate a shrimp. Use a medium-size spinning reel with good drag loaded with 20-pound mono attached to a 30-pound fluorocarbon leader connected with an Albright knot to the main fishing line.

For big kingfish and blackfin tuna, Capt. Skevington trolls heavier bucktail jigs at about 6 to 7 knots on 50-pound-class outfits loaded with 50-pound mono. He looks for kingfish anywhere from near the beach to 40 miles offshore, depending on bait location and water temperature and clarity. Skevington finds blackfin tuna in waters deeper than about 70 feet, but you can also target them over deep wrecks and around weed and tide lines.

When trolling for these pelagics, set your lines back 100 feet or more, and don't tip the jig with anything because that may make it spin, which ruins the action and twists the leader. For leader material, start with either a 80-pound fluorocarbon or 108-pound coffee-

King mackerel, locally called "kings" or "kingfish," are a prime target for anglers using a fast-moving diamond jig or bucktail.

colored steel leader, depending on what predators are hitting and their corresponding dentistry. Attach the leader to the main line with a #5 80-pound swivel.

Capt. Skevington's favorite amberjack bucktail is a 4- to 5-ounce red-and-white generic model jigged on top of wrecks in 100 or more feet of water. Drop your jig near or to the bottom, and then retrieve it with a yo-yo motion combined with fast cranking to work the jig back to the boat. In other words, lift the rod with a sharp snap and reel as you drop the tip again. Either medium-heavy conventional or spinning rods work well when rigged with 30-pound mono or braid attached to 50-pound fluorocarbon leader.

23

DRIFTING OVER LEVEL BOTTOMS

Bucktail jigs can be categorized in several ways. One obvious classification system includes those cast in shallow areas, those jigged in deep water, those drifted as a component of a rig and those that are trolled.

It's not really difficult to select a jig to match your intended fishing waters; use lighter jigs in shallow water and for small fish, and heavier jigs in deep water, strong currents and for large fish. You can also use larger or smaller jigs, when desired, if they are part of a three-way rig. One type of three-way rig is excellent for fluke fishing.

A standard three-way fluke rig consists of a fluke fly tied about 18 inches above a bucktail jig used as the bottom weight. Both are tipped with fresh bait. This is a very successful combination for drifting over sand or gravel bottoms.

Drifting is an easy and productive system of fishing for bottom dwellers. Fluke, also called summer flounder, are one of the most popular species on the East Coast and the number one target when slow drifting inshore waters. These large flatfish are excellent eating and fun to catch.

Bucktails are perfect lures for fluke fishing. Their appearance alone—resembling squid, which are primary fluke forage—makes bucktail jigs enticing. Add to that their quality of a heavy, drift-efficient jig with flowing body material presenting an irresistible action and you have a perfect fluking lure.

Ask ten fluke pros what's the deadliest summer-flounder rig, and you'll likely hear ten different answers—many experts customize their fluke set-ups to various degrees. However, commercially tied fluke rigs work well, too. The truth is that all fluke rigs, homemade or commercially manufactured, will produce big flatties when the fish are numerous and the bite is on, but the debates arise when fish are scattered or fussy, and that's when one fluke rig may outfish another.

Fluke rigs vary primarily in lure and bait presentation, but they also have similar components in their basic design. Almost every configuration has a heavy, bottom-dragging lure—usually a bucktail jig of 2 to 6 ounces—tied about 12 to 18 inches below a three-way swivel often using sacrificial mono leader of 20-pound test.

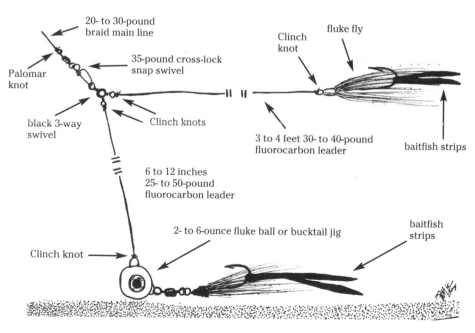

Example of 3-Way Fluke Rig

The purpose of the light leader is to be strong enough to boat a fluke but be weaker than the main line so only the bottom lure is lost if irretrievably snagged. Many anglers, however, are willing to risk losing an entire rig so as not to worry about breaking off a large fluke due to insufficient leader strength.

Another leader, often fluorocarbon of 25- to 50-pound test and 24 to 36 inches long, is tied to the second eye of the three-way swivel. Attached to the opposite end of this leader is a soft plastic squid imitation or big bucktail or Mylar fly, which trails a couple of feet behind and above the bottom-dragging jig during a drift. Both hooks are almost always tipped or sweetened with a squid strip, fish-belly strip and/or small baitfish. This is called a three-way rig.

Although white is the most popular color for fluke lures and flies, flatfish can be picky. Experts often change lure colors until they find the one producing on a given day. Other popular colors include chartreuse, yellow, green, natural and pink.

Many commercially-tied fluke rigs feature abundant "jewelry." A common theory in fluke-rig design is to use as many attractants near the hook as possible. Beads, spinners and colorful tubes are routinely strung ahead of hooks like holiday decorations to increase the offering's visibility.

A second school of thought, however, is to use a cleaner rig with minimal ornamentation. Anglers who favor the plain look claim too much flash frightens fish. The fact of the matter is if fluke are present and feeding they'll probably strike either type of offering equally well. But if they're fussy you'll need to experiment.

One example of a custom fluke rig is that of Kerry Douton, captain of the charterboat *Dot-E-Dee* and owner of J&B Tackle in Niantic, Connecticut. His favorite three-way rig is weighted with a 4-ounce Blue Shad SPRO Bucktail Jig. The jig features a large, supersharp Gamakatsu hook covered by a thick plume of blue, white and black bucktail tied into a shiny, baitfish-painted lead head with large eyes.

When hopped along the bottom, a SPRO jig body stays almost parallel to the ocean floor, thus maintaining a more natural appearance. SPRO accomplishes this balance point by precise placement of the attachment ring, which is more centrally located than on most other bucktail jigs.

Capt. Douton runs about 12 inches of 30-pound fluorocarbon from the SPRO jig to a three-way swivel. From the second swivel eye comes about 3 feet of the 30-pound fluorocarbon which is tied to a large, blue-and-white Deceiver-style fly. He then tips both the fly and the jig with squid or bait strips. The third eye of the three-way swivel is attached to the main line, which is usually 20- to 30-pound super braid.

The advantage of super braid in fluke fishing is significant and worth the extra money. The high sensitivity and thinner diameter allows the angler to feel the slightest strike while reducing line angle due to drag.

Not everybody prefers SPRO jigs for fluke fishing. Any standard bucktail jig will work, provided the color is bright and the weight is heavy enough to hold bottom given the depth, current and drift speed. Naturally, anytime you drag a weight along the bottom it will eventually snag, therefore, many experts like a jig head with an upturned nose such as the banana-head style, which tends to sled over the bottom more easily without digging in.

Most fluke fishing is done from a drifting boat. As you drift, work the bucktail along a sand and/or pebble bottom with a fairly slow yo-yo jigging stroke. Lift your rod tip about 2 feet, and then slowly lower the rod to allow the jig to sink back to the bottom. Always maintain contact with the bucktail, never creating slack in the line. You may let the lure drag bottom for a short time and then begin the cycle again. Strikes often occur on the drop or as the lure sits or drags on the bottom. Keep your hooks sharp and be prepared to strike swiftly on a hit.

Fluke usually like smooth, sandy bottoms. But they also inhabit drop-offs, shoals, channels and hook-snagging broken bottom containing scattered rocks. Other obstacles, like lobster traps or shellfish beds, are other causes of lost tackle. That means you should carry a variety of jig weights for the conditions and in sufficient numbers in case you lose a few.

In addition to the standard bucktail and SPRO jigs are relatively new lures known as fluke bombs, fluke balls, silver bullets or chrome bullets, which are highly productive and have become popular in recent years. The basic lure design consists of a 1- to 12-ounce chromed or enamel-painted lead ball with a hook attached to a swivel, which is anchored to an attachment ring molded into the lead ball. The hook is dressed with natural bucktail hair or synthetic fibers to which strands of Flashabou, silver Mylar or Krystalflash is added for sparkle. In other words, it's simply a large bucktail fly attached to a shiny, round lead sinker via a swivel.

A second metal attachment ring is embedded in the ball almost opposite the swivel's attachment ring and is used for the line. Amazingly plain in design, this heavy ball anchors the three-way rig and uses its fluttering, spinning bucktail fly to attract fluke. As with all other jigging techniques, use the lightest weight possible for the ball.

You can fish the fluke ball the same way you would a bucktail jig as described above, but the ball also catches plenty of fish when simply dragged along the bottom. The fluke ball can be fished alone or as an anchor lure for a three-way rig. Just like any bucktail jig, the fluke ball will catch other types of fish, including cod, bluefish, stripers, sea bass, sea trout and weakfish.

Although the practice is more time consuming, many charter captains agree with the importance of changing rigs when the bite is off. They constantly experiment with combinations of color, size, shape, scent, bait, weight and leader length until they find the formula for a successful trip. It's important to realize that the color or configuration that works one day may not work the next.

Unlike winter flounder, which are sedentary, fluke are striking predators that will sometimes follow prey or a baited hook toward the surface. The lesson here, according to fluke experts Capt. Jim Kaczynski and Capt. Jim Maturo, who fish fluke from the *Aqua Gem* out of Pt. Judith, Rhode Island, is that when retrieving a rig to check your bait, reel in slowly enough to allow a pursuing fish the chance to grab the hook. Although it saves time, they believe an angler should never reel in as fast as normal. Instead, use a steady pace and stop several times on the way up, especially in shallow water. Even dropping the

From left to right, Capt. Jim Kaczynski, Capt. Jim Maturo and Maggie Migdalski show off part of their fluke catch while using three-way rigs off the Rhode Island coast.

bucktail jig back a few feet will sometimes prompt an aggressive strike. The combination of your drift speed and slow reeling will create the appearance of a prey trying to escape.

Another variation of the stop-and-drop is harder to master but is deadly on fluke only moderately interested in feeding: If you miss a strike, immediately free-spool your bucktail back for about 10 to 15 seconds. This gives lazy fluke the impression that they stunned or killed their prey. The method requires a subtle feel because some of these fish won't suddenly strike and run. Instead, they inhale the dropped-back bait and just hang there with it in their mouth until you feel pressure and set the hook.

Boat handling also comes into play when fluke fishing. One method, commonly used in southern regions, is to anchor or slow drift near shellfish beds with a bag of ground chum hanging near the bottom. Cast downtide of the chum flow with a single, small lead-head bucktail jig tipped with a bait strip. Let the jig settle, and then gradually retrieve it with a slow twitch so it bounces along the bottom. This often results in catches of weakfish, striped bass, bluefish, southern flatfish or sea trout.

A second technique, popular in the Northeast, is to drift channel edges or deep-water sand bottoms with any variation of a three-way rig described above. Critical to drifting success is to pick the right conditions. An ideal situation is a light breeze moving in the same direction as the current. This keeps your boat drifting in the desired direction with speed for sufficient lure movement.

On the other hand, an opposing tide and wind offset each other and may either hold you motionless or move you with the wind. Fluke face into the tide to enhance their oxygen intake and to ambush prey moving down-current and towards them. Therefore, your best drift presentation will come with a prevailing current—your baits will approach the fluke face first, rather than from behind.

Other important elements of successful fishing include a depthfinder and GPS unit. Depthfinders, nicknamed fishfinders, won't actually locate fluke because of their low profile; however, bottom electronics do show slopes, basins, drop-offs and edges that fluke inhabit. A GPS unit is very handy for retracing the track of your drift after finding a productive area where you landed several keeper-size fish. In smaller boats, a short length of heavy chain tied to a rope and dragged on the bottom is helpful to slow your drift if the wind or current are too strong. This trick can also attract fluke because it ruffles the bottom and stirs up forage.

Almost any rod will catch fluke and southern flounder, but certain rod-and-reel combinations are much more effective than others for detecting a flatfish's subtle bite when the flattie deftly inhales a hook. The proper rod rating and action is also important for fighting and landing flatfish because of their paper-thin mouths and vigorous head shakes. That explains why many big fish are lost at the surface with an unforgiving rod.

One outfit the pros use and recommend is a 7-foot medium-light rod with a soft tip, but stiff backbone. Another similar outfit is a 6½-foot rod with a medium fast action rated for ¾ to 1¼-ounces. Fiberglass, graphite and composite rods all work well and are personal preference according to the feel you like and your budget. Match your rod with any high-quality baitcasting reel with a levelwind system, which is helpful in deep water situations. Good reel examples include a Penn 975LD or Shimano Tekota 500.

Spool your reel with 20- to 30-pound super braid for its high sensitivity and narrow diameter, which is extremely important for minimum resistance in deep water and during fast drifts. Fluke have keen eyes, and that's why most pros use fluorocarbon leader material, rather than mono, in the 30- to 50-pound range. Use a uni-to-uni knot combination for tying super line to similar diameter mono or fluorocarbon, taking four to five turns with the leader but seven to eight turns with the braid. You can also use an Albright knot for tying braid to leader material of a larger diameter. For step-by-step knot tying, click on at www.animatedknots.com.

Sea bass inhabit some of the same environments as fluke do, but they feed on a wider forage base including crab, young lobster, shrimp, mollusks, baitfish and squid. Because of this varied diet, large sea bass respond well to both diamond jigs and bucktails, but one of the best jigs for sea bass is a fluke ball.

You can work a fluke ball for sea bass the same way you would fish a bucktail for them, which is bouncing it with big hops along the bottom. However, it will also produce sea bass by moving it with short strokes or twitches of the rod tip so it barely bumps bottom. Simply dragging the ball along the bottom as you slow-drift, like when fluke fishing, also works. Single hooks perform best to reduce bottom snags, and any bucktail will catch more sea bass if you tip the hook with a fresh baitfish or squid strip.

24

DEEP DRIFTING THREE-WAY RIGS AND TROLLING WIRE LINE

Deep water and fast current can conspire to make drifting and deep jigging difficult. In these situations, three-way rigs or wire line trolling are two techniques that can get the job done.

Three Way Rigs

In large rips, such as the famous Race at the entrance of Long Island Sound, it's impossible to fish a small, standard bucktail by itself in swift waters reaching 90 to 180 feet deep. Holding along the bottom would require a bucktail with a massive lead head of 10 to 20 ounces, especially on a full-moon tide. A solution is to fish a light bucktail—matching the size of local baitfish and offering good action—by carrying it to the bottom with a heavy sinker tied to a three-way swivel, which is another variation of a three-way rig. The purpose of the sinker is simply to tend the bottom and know how deep your rig is working.

Because of the harsh fishing conditions in big rips, traditional three-way tackle traditionally consisted of heavy- to extra-heavy action boat rods rigged to workhorse reels like Penn 4/0 Senators loaded with 40- to 60-pound mono. Sixteen- to 24-ounce sinkers were necessary to keep the thick mono fishing vertically, but super braid lines, which are thinner and stronger, have created a new era in three-way-rig drifting, allowing the use of lighter gear because of reduced current drag. The weight of the lead sinker can be reduced by half, which allows anglers to use correspondingly lighter rods and smaller reels. The new set-up makes three-way drifting more sporting and enjoyable because the tackle weighs less, and anglers can fight just the fish rather than fight the fish plus the weight of a massive sinker.

One of the pioneers of light-tackle fishing in deep rips is Capt. Kerry Douton, of the charterboat *Dot-E-Dee* in Niantic, Connecticut.

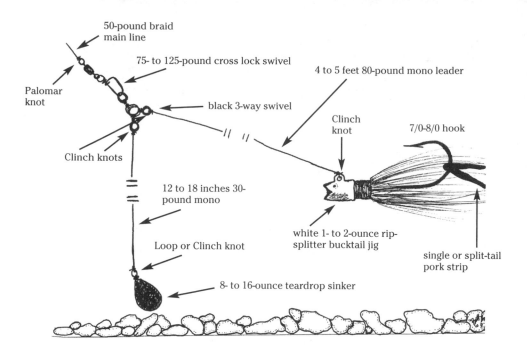

Example of 3-Way Bucktail Rig

His three-way rigs consist of a 1¼-ounce bucktail jig fixed to an 8/0 hook. Jigs of that weight are usually constructed with a 6/0 hook, but Douton's shop, J&B Tackle, orders the larger, special-made hooks because they hold better on big fish and don't straighten under pressure. You can fish a slightly heavier jig, but larger jigs lose their swimming action when the current slows.

If you only have access to smaller rips in your area, try the same three-way-configuration with an appropriate sinker and replace the lead-head bucktail with a plastic-head shovelnose driftweight bucktail. The lightweight plastic head prevents the jig from sagging below the sinker and not holding out horizontally in the current or "swimming" properly.

Select white or bright-colored jigs during the day and black or purple bucktails at night. Tipping any jigs with pork rind or a plastic tail makes them appear more enticing. Popular pork rind colors are white, chartreuse or yellow, but red-and-white seems to be the best and most consistent color pattern during the day, while you should again choose black for nighttime. Pork rind is important because it flutters seductively in the current and simulates a baitfish's beating tail or a squid's pulsing tentacles. The angler doesn't impart any other action to the lure with his rod or reel.

A bucktail jig tipped with a pork rind (visible against and beneath the fish's lower jaw) and tied to a three-way rig is an excellent system for catching bluefish and striped bass in rips otherwise too deep to fish without additional weight.

The actual fishing method is to run uptide from the shoal or reef while watching your depthfinder. Stop at the point where the slope levels to flat bottom. Throw the throttle into neutral and immediately free spool your rig to the bottom. Take two to three reel turns up to clear the rocks, and then hold your outfit still. Every time you feel a bump, which is usually the sinker striking bottom, immediately lift your rod tip and take two or three more turns in. This either clears bottom or sets the hook on a fish.

In some rips, with the current at or near peak, it's sometimes necessary to let line out as you lose the feel of the bottom even when the depth decreases. This condition occurs when the boat is drifting at a faster rate than your rig below. Along some reefs and shoals, striped bass will hold behind the structure. Once you clear the peak you'll need to let line out and drift into the rip itself as the structure deepens again. Only do this if you have a seaworthy boat that can handle the waves in the rip line. Repeat successful drifts by using electronics, triangulation or, in smaller rips, a retrievable, homemade marker made from an empty bleach bottle with suitable line and weight attached.

To create a three-way rig, tie a 1- to 2-ounce rip-splitter-style bucktail to 5 feet of 80-pound mono leader fixed to one eye of a heavy-duty three-way swivel. Tie 18 to 24 inches of 30-pound mono from a 6- to 12-ounce sinker tied to the second eye on the three-way swivel. The lighter mono acts as a sacrificial leader in case the sinker snags bottom. The light line breaks and spares the rest of your expensive rig and line.

If you do hang bottom, act fast and point the rod directly toward the line, tighten the drag and put your thumb on the spool. Hold the tension firm until the sinker lets go or the leader parts. Some anglers try to yank off the snag with the rod, but that doesn't work well. The rod flexes and just buries the sinker deeper in the rocks, and it's an easy way to break your rod. Do this immediately because the boat is drifting; otherwise, the diagonal line angle will increase and you'll lose the rig. On smaller rips with light boat traffic it's possible to run back uptide and try to pull the sinker free from the opposite direction. Use great care not to snap a rod or tangle the line in your prop when attempting this maneuver.

For tackle, use high-quality conventional reels with or without a levelwind. Some experts feel that levelwind reels restrict the speed of the drop, thereby letting the line float in a stiff current before the rig reaches bottom. Others disagree and successfully use high-quality levelwinds for drifting bucktails. Purchase reels with heavy-duty gears and drags made by major manufacturers like Penn and Shimano in sizes equivalent to a 2/0 or 3/0.

Load reels with 30-pound Dacron backing and top-shot them with 150 yards of 30- to 50-pound spectra line. Attach the reels to 6½- to 7-foot, medium-heavy rods in the 17- to 40-pound range.

Wire-Line Trolling

Wire-line trolling hasn't changed much in the Northeast—the region where it is most commonly used—since its inception about 75 years ago. The reason is because wire lining is the most effective and basic method for dragging bucktail-type jigs in front of large striped bass, bluefish and weakfish.

These predators—especially bass and weakfish—spend most of their time prowling the bottom and prefer an easy meal swept past their nose rather than working for their food by chasing it up through the water column. That's because their instincts guide them to consume the most nutrient rich and easiest forage available while expending the least amount of energy.

Other deep-trolling techniques do exist, of course, and include planer boards, downriggers and in-line sinkers, but wire line is faster, cleaner and easier to use, especially over rocky structure where depths change quickly. Wire has other advantages, too: Its zero stretch enables penetrating hook-sets on bony-jawed critters like big bluefish, and it rarely tangles when making tight trolling turns. Wire line also stays down and out of the way on the second outfit when fighting a fish on the first. Unlike planers or downriggers, wire-lined lures run directly to the rod, allowing them to swim properly and be worked with the rod tip for life-like action.

Contrary to what some anglers think—and despite the IGFA's rule that it doesn't recognize world records landed on wire line—wire has nothing to do with line strength or abrasion resistance. In fact, the most popular wire-line rating is only 40- to 50-pound test. The sole purpose of trolling with wire, usually made of stainless steel or a nickel alloy like monel, is to sink lures to the bottom at depths of 20 to 50 feet or more. If you attempted the same trolling technique with braid or mono, you would need at least double, if not triple, the amount of line behind your boat.

In southern New England and off the Mid Atlantic, big fish prowl deep reefs, shoals and channels during midday hours and when sea surface temperatures rise above their comfort level. The best place to find the perfect combination of fishing conditions—depth, shelter, current and forage—is in rips that form over structure or along bottom contours.

To locate likely rips near you, look over a local chart and pinpoint areas where the depth rises and falls abruptly. Rip lines make convenient and precise roadmaps along which to troll. During slower tide periods a parallel trolling pattern is possible; however, when the current is running hard you may need to tow diagonally into it or stem the tide.

Stemming the tide means slowly motoring diagonally into the flow of a strong current. That way, the boat isn't swept sideways over the reef and you can pull your lures along in the strike zone. Most days the zone is just ahead of the rip in the sweet spot, but occasionally the strike zone is on top or just behind the structure. Current velocity and the presence of bait, coupled with your experience on each reef, determine the best location on a given day.

Generally, fishing is best during peak current flow, and the fishing typically improves around the times of full and new moons. Early mornings, late afternoons and overcast days often produce well on large striped bass, which prefer low-light conditions, although schoolie bass, bluefish and weakfish feed all day under bright skies.

Maintaining your jig at the right depth is extremely important for catching fish over structure. If a lure is trolled higher than a few feet off the bottom, lazy predators either won't see it or won't make the effort to chase it. Most hits occur when the lure occasionally bumps along the reef. This is when proper trolling technique pays off.

Reefs, shoals and bars are rarely a consistent depth. Anglers who troll their jigs at only one depth will either cruise them above the strike zone or constantly drag or hang bottom. The pros, on the other hand, make rapid adjustments to depth changes by releasing or retrieving wire as needed.

When trolling properly, your jig should hit bottom occasionally. That's how you know your lure is in the strike zone. The disturbance also seems to attract fish, but once your jig starts constantly bumping bottom, immediately take about five fast turns in. If you're still bumping, take another five. If you're trolling along and haven't felt anything for awhile, slowly let line out until the jig makes occasional contact again. You can tell if your jig has been bumping bottom by the appearance of the jig head, which will have paint worn off and/or a flattened nose. Maintaining proper lure depth is also easier if you keep an eye on the boat's depthfinder to track the changes in depth, remembering that the lure is trailing up to 300 feet behind your current depth reading.

Parachute-style bucktail jigs fished deep with wire line is one of the most effective ways to coax lazy, midday striped bass and weakfish to strike. These outfits are rigged and ready to deploy in a nearshore rip in the Northeast. Two rods are trolled at a time, the third is a spare in case a wire line breaks from fatigue or a kink.

Correct trolling speed is crucial for catching big fish like striped bass. Power your boat at or under about 2 to 2½ knots or 2½ to 3 mph, which is the optimum trolling speed to impart action to jigs and keep them skimming over a reef without having to deploy excessive amounts of wire line. Check your travel rate with both GPS and paddlewheel units to correct for the influence of current speed, if necessary.

Any leadhead bucktail jig will work when wire lining. They are perfect deep-trolling lures for this application because they take the abuse of a rough bottom and are easy to set out, fish, retrieve and unhook, but the most effective of the leadhead jigs are the group of lures called "parachute" jigs, such as those made by Andrus. These jigs aren't true bucktails because they're tied with synthetic fibers. The artificial fibers are colorful, longer and much more durable than natural hairs. Unlike traditional bucktail jigs, parachute manufacturers attach the fibers facing both forward and rearward, thereby creating an enticing action that's difficult for predators to resist.

A parachute jig has little or no action by itself. To induce strikes, you need to give your parachute a jigging motion. Facing the stern, hold your rod tip down to the water (either off the side or over the stern) with the guides facing the bow. Sweep the rod back (toward the bow) with short, rapid strokes, causing the forward-facing or

Parachute jigs tied with nylon fibers facing both forward and rearward are an excellent simulation of squid. Tipping the hook with a pork rind finishes the presentation by representing the tentacles. This lure is a 3-ounce Fire Fly swing-hook jig made by McKala Fishing LLC.

parachute fibers to pulsate like a swimming squid or injured baitfish. Keep the rhythm as consistent as possible because predators often time a prey's movement before striking.

When a wire-lining hook-up occurs, it's routine for some captains to continue trolling so the other angler can keep fishing and also doesn't hang bottom. You'll probably land more fish and have more fun fighting them if you lower the boat's speed (engine rpms) to idle and ask the other angler to crank in his line. Many times this speed change and retrieve prompts a second strike.

Parachute jig weights generally range from 2 to 6 ounces, but use the lightest jig possible to achieve the best action and reduce snags, which usually means jigs in the 2- to 4-ounce range. When you're fishing two rods, use the same weight on both outfits to reduce tangles during turns and to keep equal amounts of wire out. Size 8/0 hooks are ideal size for large bluefish, stripers and weakfish.

Some pros, like Capt. Ned Kittredge aboard the *Watch Out*, change their factory-installed hooks to stainless steel to prevent rust and avoid discoloring the nylon fibers. Once sharpened, stainless steel also holds a point longer than standard hooks, but always keep a sharpener handy to touch-up hook points dulled on rough bottoms.

Swing-style hooks are better than fixed hooks because they give more action and hold better in a fish's mouth where they reduce the leverage the predator can apply against the jig. The most popular jig colors are chartreuse or chartreuse-and-white. For more action tip the jig with a red-and-white pork rind like the very popular Uncle Josh No. 70-S Striper Strip, which simulates a baitfish's beating tail or a squid's tentacles.

Spool your reel about half full with 80-pound Dacron backing and top-shot it with 300 feet of 40-pound to 50-pound (or .025 diameter) wire. You can use a small barrel swivel to attach the wire line to the backing and to the leader. Shots of wire line are commonly sold in some tackle shops pre-rigged with swivels at each end. According to Capt. Al Anderson aboard the *Prowler*, swivels can part when fighting big fish. He suggests using a nail knot instead of a swivel, which passes easily through the guides and holds securely. Anderson folds the tag end of the wire over to form a loop and ties the leader to the wire with a nail knot. To neatly finish the knot he barrel wraps the remaining tag end of the wire back over the standing portion so there is no sharp edge. Along the Jersey Coast and in Chesapeake Bay, the Albright is a favorite connection. Most areas along the coast favor a 15-foot length of 50-pound mono leader, which gives the lure a more natural appearance and acts as a shock absorber when fighting bigger fish giving violent head shakes. If you're fishing in very rocky areas or expecting a lot of toothy bluefish, add 4 feet of 80-pound mono abrasion leader in front of the lure, using a blood knot for the leader-to-leader connection and a simple clinch knot for the leader-to-jig connection.

Wire line must be marked at increments for accurate depth reference. The rule-of-thumb is to pay out 10 diagonal feet of wire for every vertical foot of depth. Typically, wire comes pre-marked with colored vinyl tape. A common setup for a 300-foot shot of line is orange tape at the first 100-foot mark, followed thereafter by red, white and blue at 50-foot increments. Accurately marked line is important for fast line setting, and so you can deploy the same length of line again after having success. Stainless steel is the most popular wire choice because it's the least expensive, but it's springy and some pros like the softer monel and the new inconel.

On one hand, wire line tackle can be just basic conventional-style gear, while on the other hand it can be fairly specialized. Although any medium-heavy boat-rod-and-conventional-reel combo will do for a couple trips a year, the use of the right tackle will prevent long-term damage to your rod, reel and line. Wire lining requires a rod that imparts good action to the lure yet has a substantial backbone and durable guides.

A 6½- to 7-foot rod with a soft tip and stiff butt section rated for 20- to 40-pound line is a good all-round choice. Long rods allow a greater jigging sweep with less effort. The soft tip gives a 'chute a smooth action while being gentle on the wire so it doesn't weaken prematurely. Carbide guides are necessary to prevent grooving, and some experts like a roller guide at the tip for reduced friction.

The standard wire-line-trolling reel in the Northeast is the Penn 113HLW 4/0 Senator, however, such a large reel isn't necessary for inshore fishing over shallow reefs or along estuary shoals like river mouths. In such situations, the lighter, smaller 112H 3/0 Senator is ideal. Other similar reels, such as Shimano's TLD 15 work equally well.

One word of caution: Wire line is unwieldy in the hands of novices. Beginners must take great care to keep a thumb on the spool and tension on the line at all times to prevent severe backlashes and bird nests.

Jerry Martin admires his big striper taken on a 3-ounce parachute jig trolled in front of a rip while using 40-pound wire line affixed to 15 feet of 50-pound mono leader. This is a chartreuse-and-white jig tipped with a red-and-white pork strip.

IV
Concluding Tips

25

TWELVE TIPS FOR LANDING YOUR FISH

Fighting a fish with a jig in its mouth differs from fighting or landing fish caught on a fly, plastic lure or bait hook because of the unusual forces applied by a heavy, swinging weight. As a result, anglers need use special care to boat a fish without losing it, damaging the vessel or injuring someone onboard. These 10 tips will allow you to more safely and successfully land fish on large bucktails or vertical jigs.

1. Control your rod pumping. When cranking a big fish up from the depths, most captains and mates recommend you just reel steadily and don't pump the rod with alternating bursts of reeling, as you would do when fighting a big-game fish. Although this may be more taxing to the angler and to the reel, it prevents instances of lost tension when briefly dropping the rod tip before reeling starts. Less tension means a loose hook and lost fish. There's no reason, however, you can't pump up a big cod, grouper or yellowtail from the depths, but only do so if you are experienced with this method and can perform perfect transitions from lifting to reeling. The bottom line is this: Whether you choose to fight a fish with a static rod and straight reeling or by pumping and reeling, keep a bend in your rod tip at all times to maintain firm contact with the fish.

2. Adjust your drag. In deep water or when a big fish is making a long run away from the boat, your drag will increase significantly as the diameter of your spooled line decreases. If you fear the hook may pull or the line may break, start backing off on the drag in small increments. You can tighten the drag again, if necessary, after you've recovered a lot of lost line. When the fish approaches the gaff or the net, however, it's usually a good idea to slightly back off on the drag again. A sudden surge at boat side can rip out a hook or part a leader.

3. Handle jumping fish. When a fly-rod-hooked tarpon jumps, for example, the angler is supposed to "bow" to the fish. In other words, he backs off on the pressure by instantly lowering the fly rod to the fish. However, the opposite is true with jigs. When a fish, such as a bluefish, jumps with a jig dangling from its mouth you should lean

Capt. Ned Kittredge shows how diamond jig bodies make a great handhold for lifting and unhooking your catch.

Back off on your drag when a big fish nears the boat to prevent parting the line or tearing out the hook during a sudden run.

back with the rod to keep tension on the jig; otherwise, the fish's violent head shakes will create jig momentum and allow the fish to throw the hook. Keeping tension on the jig prevents it from flailing in the fish's mouth. Circle hooks will help prevent thrown lures.

4. Don't lift with the rod. Never lift a fish from the water with the rod. That's a sure way to break your tackle, snap a line or rip out the hook. Remember, when you lift a fish from the water you lift its full weight; when it's in the water, however, a fish is weightless.

5. Control thrashing. At the end of a battle try to prevent the fish from thrashing on the surface because that's an easy way to cut a leader with sharp teeth or wrench out the hook by leveraging it against the weight of the jig. A thrashing fish also makes it more difficult for a mate to gaff or net your catch, especially from the high sides of a party boat. That means keep tension on the line, but not excessive tension.

6. Ease rod tension. If a friend or mate leans overboard to grab the leader of a spent fish, ease off on the rod bend and line tension. Continuing to hold the fish hard at the boat with a deeply bent rod means the gear is "loaded," like a bow ready to release an arrow, and if the jig pulls out it may rocket into the cockpit or strike the person leaning overboard.

To best help a mate, keep your line tight so the fish—like this lingcod—doesn't shake its head and throw the hook or swim around other anglers' lines. But don't continue to apply maximum rod bend in case the jig flies out. *Photo by Doug Olander.*

7. Give a fish some distance. Whenever possible don't let a tired fish slide right up against your hull. As the fish gives its final fight it will shake its head and often whack the hull with the jig, sometimes chipping the gel coat. Try to hold it about a half rod length from the side.

8. Control the sinker. When boating a fish caught on a three-way rig featuring a heavy weight, be wary of a sometimes wildly swinging sinker, made worse by the vessel pitching as it drifts into a rip. The sinker acts as a fast-moving pendulum and can knock an angler in the face or chip the gel coat off the side of your boat. One way to "soften the blow" is to dip your sinkers in liquid rubber during the off season, which will help avoid damaging your fiberglass. You can even color code them by weight; for example, red is 8 ounces, blue is 10 ounces and so forth.

9. Lift with the jig. Unlike other lures, such as big plugs with two or three sets of treble hooks, vertical jig bodies provide a convenient and sturdy handhold for you to grab the lure and lift a fish from the water. Use special care in doing this if the jig has two dangling assist hooks as featured on Butterfly-style lures. If only one hook is in the fish's mouth, the other may be swinging freely.

These fishing partners demonstrate good technique after hooking two bluefish on bucktails fished off three-way rigs. Hold the leader and sinker to help control the chaos and to safely lift fish from the water without using the rod.

10. Get the fish out of the water. When lifting a toothy critter like a bluefish from the water by holding the jig, use great caution and precise timing until the fish has cleared the surface. If you hold the lure for a moment too long while the fish's tail is in the water it can propel itself upward and slice your fingers with its teeth. Once the fish is completely out of the water, however, it can shake and flop around a lot but can't push itself upward to your hand—so hold on tightly!

11. Control boated fish. If you value the gel coat on your boat's interior, don't lift a fish from the water and drop it on the deck. A strong fish will shake hard enough to chip your fiberglass or whack your ankles with the heavy metal jig it's flailing. If a fish falls on the deck, however, throw a wet rag over its head. Preventing it from seeing usually calms most fish, and this is a common technique used by taggers.

12. Secure your jigs. When running with rigged rods in rough seas, snuggly secure your jigs against the rods or the boat—Velcro bands work well. A heavy jig held in place only by hooking it into a rod guide-post will bounce free and swing wildly, possibly hooking someone in the face, chipping the gel coat or cracking a windshield.

26

FIFTEEN TIPS FOR
PHOTOGRAPHING YOUR CATCH

Although there's nothing wrong with keeping a few fish for the table, much of the future of recreational fishing depends on conservation and proper management of our resources. Therefore, I thought it best to change the final chapter from "how to care for your catch" (gut, fillet, chill, cook, freeze and thaw) to "how to photograph your catch," so you can save the memories, but still release the fish.

It takes a lot of thought and effort to take photos that look good and really show the beauty of your catch. By following the 15 tips in this chapter, you can wow your friends and improve the quality of your photo album.

1. Take your camera with you. That may sound obvious, but bring your camera on every trip. Sooner or later somebody will catch a big one you'll want to photograph. Photos taken on the water with a fresh fish look the best. Have you ever noticed what back-at-home photos look like? Invariably they show gutted, faded, stiff fish held in front of a garage, pickup truck or kitchen sink—and those fish are pretty hard to revive and release. Don't forget to keep the camera loaded with a fresh memory card or film and new batteries.

2. Tell the whole story. Don't just wait for the "hero shot" of your friend grinning with his prize catch. People looking at fishing photos—especially fishermen—are interested in more than just the end result.

Take a few shots at sunrise as the boat is pulling away from the dock. Or record the birds working over a surface blitz. Certainly photograph the battle, the landing and the releasing of fish, but you will need to sacrifice some fishing time in order to capture the most memorable images of each trip.

3. Take a lot of shots. The more photos you shoot the better your chances are of nailing a great one. A good rule-of-thumb is the more

Al Buchman does a great job posing with this fish by looking at the fish, holding it in a diagonal position and clearly displaying the tackle and diamond jig. Use a fill-flash to illuminate dark areas such as a face shaded by a cap.

people that are in the photo the more shots you should take. That's because of the increased chance that someone will have his eyes closed or a stupid look on his face. Burning through more images also increases your odds of sharp and properly exposed photos.

4. Have someone doing something. Instead of photographing that worn-out scenario of the angler grinning at the camera and shoving the fish toward the lens, have him doing something to appear more candid. The simplest trick is to tell him to look at the fish (as he would if there was no camera), but be sure his cap doesn't block his eyes. If two people are in the photo, have one person showing the fish to the other person. The angler(s) could also pose with the fish by landing, unhooking, measuring, tagging, weighing or releasing it.

5. Watch the background. Don't include something in the background that detracts from your photo. For example, look for parts of other people, beverage cans, buckets or rags. Be sure a rod doesn't appear to protrude from an angler's head like a unicorn, and keep your horizons level.

6. Use different angles. Most pictures are taken at eye level. You can increase the interest in your photos by shooting up or down at

Jerry Martin and Maggie Migdalski look at each other instead of the camera to best create a candid image. Set up your shot and then say something funny to get real expressions of laughter rather than a staged look. A fill-flash eliminates shadows from the caps and highlights sparkles on the fish.

your subject. For instance, kneel on the deck while the angler stands with the fish. Shooting up at the fish is a unique angle, and it often makes the fish look larger. Or have the angler kneel on the deck while you stand. On larger boats, it's possible to shoot down from the bridge or from the steps leading to a bridge. Use great caution, however, when attempting to stand on a bow cover, poling platform or seat. That's an easy way to take a tumble, which probably isn't good for you or your camera. Another fresh angle is to lean over the gunnel and photograph along the boat side as a fish is slowly lifted or released. But watch the salt spray!

7. Avoid hard shadows. A "hard" shadow is one which blackens a portion of the subject, usually cast by overhead sunshine. Caps and hats are the most common cause of hard shadows on sunny days. There are two easy ways to avoid this problem: The first, and most obvious, is to ask the angler to tip up or remove his cap. The second, if your camera is capable, is to use a fill-flash by setting your camera to fire the flash during bright conditions when it's not normally required. The flash lightens or removes distracting shadows on bright days and makes fish sparkle on dull, overcast days.

8. Include the tackle. Rather than taking all your shots the same way, that is, with a person holding just a fish, try including some tackle. This tip makes photos more varied and interesting, and it also helps rekindle fond memories years later. Try having the angler hold the rod across the fish, or leave the diamond jig in the its mouth. Other ideas include shooting close-ups of just the reel and jig or a spread of colorful bucktails in a tackle box. An especially nice way to photograph a close-up of a favorite jig is to lay it against the fish's side or shoot it hanging from a fish's mouth.

9. Concentrate on composition. The majority of snapshots show a person too far away and with a lot of "dead" or empty space around him. Sometimes, feet, hands or tops of heads are cut off. Instead, move closer (or zoom in) to the subject and fill the frame with the main subject. Another tendency of amateurs is to always hold the camera horizontally. This makes for monotonous pages in the photo album and often frames shots poorly. For example, an angler who is standing and holding a large fish under the gill plate is a vertical subject. If you turn the camera on end to shoot vertically you'll reduce the amount of dead space around the angler and fish. You'll also be able to zoom in more or step closer without cutting off the fish's tail.

10. Position the fish in a variety of ways. Rather than always having the model hold the fish the same way, try various poses with the fish. An open-mouth, head-on shot of a big fish is a real attention grab-

Create non-traditional poses to capture the best results in your photos. Here the guys are both looking at the fish while the angler extends his arms in a candid show of celebration.

Showing the tackle and incorporating action into your shots requires practice, patience, precise focus and a fast shutter speed. The fill-flash used here adds brightness and sparkle on this overcast day.

ber. Try lifting the fish about two-thirds out of the water and shoot the photo as if it were just being landed or released. Or hold the fish at a diagonal across the angler's body with the fish's head as high as the angler's. Remember to tell the angler to look at the fish's head.

In these days of conservation, avoid photos of dead fish piled on the deck, dock or in the cooler. Emphasize the quality of the experience, not the quantity of the kill. To that end, keep your fish in the water—not flopping around on the hot deck—while someone digs out and sets up the camera. Take the photos fast and get the fish back into the ocean.

11. Focus on the fish. Since a fish is almost always the subject of a fishing photo, focus on it, not the angler. More specifically, you should focus on the fish's eye. A typical pro photographer, for example, would frame a shot, tip the camera to lock the focus on the fish's head, and then re-frame the shot before releasing the shutter. While this sounds complicated, it only takes a moment, and your results will be far superior to just firing pictures as they come. Also be sure the fish is tilted properly to the camera. In other words, too much belly or back doesn't show much of the fish or its colors.

12. Wear colorful clothes. While most fishermen fish in faded, dark colored clothes, you'll notice that magazine photos show the anglers neatly dressed in clean, colorful attire. Carry a bright red T-shirt, jacket or cap, and ask the angler to put it on before taking a special photo. Colorful clothes also help the camera meter expose the shot properly. Anglers in black coats, denim jackets or white shirts can cause over- or under-exposed results. And while you're trying to look good, clean any blood off the fish and angler's hands before snapping that prize-winning picture.

13. Use warm light. "Warm" light is an artist's or photographer's term for the golden-rosy sunlight of early morning or late afternoon. When the sun is at a low angle it gives off a beautiful, rich light that enhances photos and rids the harsh shadows thrown by a high, midday sun. If your subject is facing (front light) a low-angle sun a fill-flash probably won't be needed. This is also a good time to experiment with back light, either with a fill-flash to brighten your subject or without a fill-flash to create a silhouette.

14. Experiment with filters. For those of you with a 35-mm (SLR) camera, experiment with filters. Filters can dramatically change your shots for relatively little investment. A clear filter is always a good idea to protect your lens from salt spray and scratches. A warming filter, such as an 81B, can help add that warm look to your photos. An 85B gives your shots a dark gold appearance, which offers nice mood light for early- or late-day silhouettes. A polarized filter, just like polarized sunglasses, reduces the glare off bright clothes, chrome jigs, fish, water and fish in the water. It also deeply enriches a blue sky.

15. Lose the sunglasses and smokes. Eyes tell the story about a person. You can better capture the joyful expression of an angler holding his big catch without his sunglasses on. Also ask anglers to put down the beer, soda, cigar or cigarette when posing. If the angler is shirtless, have him put one on. It'll add class to your pictures.

By following these 15 simple tips, you can impress your friends with your next batch of images and better relive those wonderful hours on the water for years to come.

Capture your happy angler about to release his prize catch, as Dan Martinez does here with his big false albacore. But have your camera ready—no fish is worth sacrificing for a photograph because you weren't organized.

SOURCES: BOOKS

Anderson, Al. *To Catch a Tuna*. Mystic, Connecticut: MT Publications, 1990.

Migdalski, Edward C. & Fichter, George S. *The Fresh and Salt Water Fishes of the World*. New York, New York: Greenwich House, 1976.

Muller, William A. *Fishing with Bucktails*. United States: William Muller and Drew Muller, 2005.

Olander, Douglas. *Northwest Coastal Fishing Guide*. Portland, Oregon: Frank Amato Publications, 1991.

Poveromo, George. *Cutting Edge Saltwater Fishing Tactics*. Parkland, Florida: Outdoor Associates, Inc. 2005.

Poveromo, George. *Successful Saltwater Fishing Tactics*. Parkland, Florida: Outdoor Associates, Inc. 2001.

Ross, David A. *The Fisherman's Ocean*. Mechanicsburg, Pennsylvania: Stackpole Books, 2000.

Ward, Nathalie / Center for Coastal Studies. *Stellwagen Bank*. Camden, Maine: Down East Books, 1995.

SOURCES: ONLINE

ACFishing.com. "Fish Identification." [Online] Available *www.acfishing. com/fishid/list.html*

Allard, Tim. "Fishing Line Buyer's Guide." [Online] OutdoorSite Library, Bass Pro Shops. Available *www.basspro.com/webapp/wcs/stores/servlet/CFPage?mode=article&objectID=31231&storeId=10151&catalogId=10001&langId=-1*

Anderson, Al. ALS Tagging Program, American Littoral Society. *www.americanlittoralsoc.org*

Bennett, Bryan. "Tricking Those Finicky Tuna." Alabama—Great Days Outdoors Magazine [Online] Available *www.gcomag.com/pages.php?page=05/01/03/0457288*

California Marine Recreational Fishing Regs: *www.dfg.ca.gov/marine/mapregs5.asp*

Diamond Jigs: *www.4fishin.com/Metal%20lures.htm*

Dictionary of Ichthyologic Terms: *www.briancoad.com/Dictionary/introduction.htm*

Finz. "Shimano Butterfly Jigs Versus Williams Speed Jigs, Which One is Best for Fishing?" [Online] Available *www.associatedcontent.com/article/242720/shimano_butterfly_jigs_versus_williamson.html*, May 18, 2007

Gardell, Arden. "Fishing Bucktails 101." [Online] Available *www.saltwateredge.com/info/BUCKTAIL-JIGS.html*

Goldberg, Al. "Cod Fish Rods—From Coxes Ledge to Georges Bank." [Online] Available *www.stripersonline.com/Pages/Articles/goldberg/agoldberg_codrod.shtml*

Gutman, Jeff. "Tips for Stand-Up Tuna Fishing on Party Boats." [Online] Available *www.voyagerfishing.com/html/stand-up_fishing.html*

Hook parts: *www.mustad.no/abouthooks/index.php*

John. "Dance a Little Jig." ShallowFish.com [Online] Available *http://shallowfish.com/2007/06/dance-a-little-jig/*, June 9, 2007

Kira, Gene, "Jig Mystery Resolved." [Online] Available *www.mexfish.com/ixtz/ixtz/af030512/af030512.htm*, May 12, 2003

Lemire, Patrick. "Diamond Jigs—Adaptable Imposters." Texas Fish and Game Pro's Tips *Texas Fish & Game* [Online] Available *www.fishgame.com/HowTo/ViewArticleEntry.aspx?categoryid=2&articleid=91* June 2007.

Lucanus cervus insect:
www.zin.ru/animalia/Coleoptera/eng/lucan02.htm

Malolo Blue Water Tackle, "Sumo Jigs." [Online] Available *www.malolotackle.com/pop.html*

Poveromo, George. "Going offshore requires deep-water drilling." ESPN Outdoors Fishing. [Online] Available *http://sports.espn.go.com/outdoors/fishing/news/story?id=2733868* January 18, 2007.

Provincetown Center for Coastal Studies. "Our Environment." [Online] Available *www.coastalstudies.org/what-we-do/stellwagen-bank/phytoplankton.htm*

Skipper John. "AVA Jigs" discussion. [Online] Available *www.skipperjohn.org/phpBB2/viewtopic.php?t=448&start=0&postdays=0&postorder=asc&highlight=* October 03, 2003.

Tackle, hooks: *www.meltontackle.com/commerce/manufacturer_detail.asp?group_id=119*

Tackle Manufacturers Directory (Cites name, location, website and what they're known for.)
www.southshorefishing.net/reference/tackle.htm

Tuna Identification: *www.atuna.com/species/species_datasheets.htm*

TACKLE COMPANIES CITED

Berkley Gulp!
www.berkley-fishing.com

Bridgeport Diamond and VI-KE Jigs
www.unclejosh.com

Chaos Tackle
www.chaosfishing.com

Diawa
www.daiwa.com

Do-It Molds
www.do-itmolds.com

Eagle Claw
www.eagleclaw.com

Fishbites
www.fishbites.com

Gamakatsu USA
www.gamakatsu.com

Iron Man Jigs
www.ironmanlures.com

Mustad assist hooks
www.mustad.no/assistrigs

Owner American Corp.
www.ownerhooks.com

Penn Fishing Tackle Co.
www.pennreels.com

Point Wilson Dart Jigs
www.dartjigs.com

Salas Lures
www.originalsalaslures.com

Shimano American Corp.
www.shimano.com

Tady Lure Corp.
557 Coral Ridge Pl
City of Industry, CA 91746-3032
Phone: 626-333-3358

FLUTTER/DEEP-DROP JIG MANUFACTURERS

Braid Products, Inc.
www.braidproducts.com

Daiwa
www.daiwa.com

Offshore Angler
www.basspro.com

ProFish Company
www.profishco.com

River2Sea
www.river2sea.com

Shimano
www.shimano.com

Shulure
www.shulure.com

SPRO
www.spro.com

Squid Jig Warehouse
www.squidjig.com

Tormenter Tackle
www.tormentertackle.com

Williamson Lures
www.williamsonlures.com

EXPERTS CITED

Anderson, Capt. Al: www.prowlerchartersri.com
Allen, Capt. Ralph: www.kingfisherfleet.com
Delph, Capt. Ralph: www.delphfishing.com
Douton, Capt. Kerry: www.jbtackle.com

Gutman, Capt. Jeff: www.voyagerfishing.com
Herrick, Capt. Hal: www.nantucketfishing.com
Kittredge, Capt. Ned: www.watchoutfish.com
Mola, Capt. Ricky: http://fishermansworld.tv/theStore.html
Poveromo, George: www.georgepoveromo.com
Skevington, Capt. Steve: www.paradisefishingcharters.com

SATELLITE SEA-SURFACE TEMPERATURE IMAGING
Fishman Forecasting
(228) 813-1750; www.fishmanforecasting.com.

Oceantemp Satellite Imaging
(732) 308-0883; www.oceantemp.com.

Offshore Satellite Services
(800) 827-4468; www.offshore-seatemp.com.

Roffer's Ocean Fishing Forecasting Service
(800) 677-7633; www.roffs.com.

SST Online
e-mail sstol.info@sstol.com; www.sstol.com.

Terrafin SST-VIEW
(800) 993-0939; www.terrafin.com.

striped bass 5, 13, 22, 24, 29, 42, 43, 45–52, 75, 77, 107, 115, 148, 149, 150, 151, 156, 168, 175, 176, 178, 179
summer flounder (see "fluke")
sweet spot 26, 145
swing hooks 17, 179

tarpon 22, 151, 185
temperature break 31, 61
thermocline 33, 62, 103
tides and currents 23–25, 29
tilefish 124, 125
Tormenter Chubby and Ribbonfish jigs 121
tuna 5, 9, 13, 29, 30, 31, 33, 38, 61–66, 74, 101–103, 113, 116, 126, 159

Virginia 49, 75

wahoo, 5
weakfish 5, 24, 29, 49, 52–54, 77, 148, 151, 167, 168, 175, 176, 179
West Coast 14, 79, 80, 83, 87
West Coast iron jigs 13–14
Williamson Benthos and Abyss jigs 121–122
wire leader 38, 41
wire lining 17, 175–181
wreckfish 125

yellowfin 61,
yellowtail 14, 15, 62, 79–81, 185

ABOUT THE AUTHOR

As a freelance outdoor writer and photographer, Tom Migdalski's work has appeared in numerous outdoor publications, including *Sport Fishing, Salt Water Sportsman, Saltwater Fly Fishing, Fly Fishing in Salt Waters, Eastern Fly Fishing, Gray's Sporting Journal, On The Water, Women in the Outdoors, Florida Sportsman, The Fisherman, Game & Fish, Wildfowl, Taxidermy Today, Center Console Angler, Shallow Water Angler, Fish Boats Registry, Fur-Fish-Game,* and *Shotgun Sports.* To date, he has published over 200 articles and over 700 photographs, including over 50 regional and national cover shots.

Tom's first book, *The Complete Book of Shotgunning Games,* was published in 1997. His third book, *Fishing Long Island Sound,* will be published in 2009.

Tom Migdalski was a guest outdoor expert featured on episodes of the Outdoor Life Network's (OLN) popular cable TV show *Gear Guide.* He is currently a regional-expert lecturer for *Salt Water Sportsman's* National Seminar Series with George Poveromo.

Tom is a member of the Outdoor Writers Association of America (OWAA) and holds a Master of Science degree in outdoor recreation and college teaching from Southern Connecticut State University. Tom continues at SCSU as an adjunct faculty member teaching nutrition in the Public and Community Health Department.

Since 1984, Tom has been the director of outdoor education and club sports at Yale University, where he also advises the fishing club and instructs non-credit physical education classes in deep-sea fishing, fly tying and clay target shooting. He is a certified shotgun coach, and he coaches the Yale trap and skeet team. The NRA presented him with its Outstanding Service to Collegiate Shooting Sports award in 1994.

Tom has fished the East Coast from Nova Scotia to Key West, including Iceland, New Brunswick and Montana, but he spends most of his free time fishing on Long Island Sound, where he gathers material for his books and articles. Tom lives in southern Connecticut with his wife Carol and their teenage daughter Maggie.